Get Into My Boat

My Boat

Let's Go Fishing

by

Suzanne L'Abbé

GET INTO MY BOAT
Copyright © 2012 by Suzanne L'Abbé
ALL RIGHTS RESERVED

McDougal Publishing is a ministry of The McDougal
Foundation, Inc., a Maryland nonprofit corporation dedicated
to spreading the Gospel of the Lord Jesus Christ to as many
people as possible in the shortest time possible.

Published by:

McDougal Publishing
P.O. Box 3595
Hagerstown, MD 21742-3595

www.mcdougalpublishing.com

ISBN: 978-1-884369-34-6

Printed in the United States of America
For Worldwide Distribution

Dedication

I dedicate this book:

To Jesus: I hope You like it, because it is in existence just because of You, Lord.

To my six most wonderful children: You are continually giving me love, peace and joy.

Acknowledgments

I want to give thanks to everyone who had a part to play in birthing this book:

My first typist, Donna Lynn
My editors, Dave, Margo and Michael
The two ladies who invested financially, Pat and Theresa.
The many pastors and friends who have prayed, Pastor Carol, Pastor Jeff, Pastor Johnnie, Pastor Dan, Pastor Gerrie and Pastor Dave
The Evangelical Sisterhood of Mary from Millet, Alberta, and from Darmstadt-Eberstadt, Germany
The End-Time Handmaidens Gwen Shaw, Rose, Nancy, Laurel and many others
Bernice, Pat, Theresa, Gineger, Lea, Janice, Olive, Kathleen, Gerri, Pierre, Phyllis, Janet, Margaret, Terri and Gergia.

Contents

About the Author...7

About the Title 11

Endorsements..13

Foreword by Gwen Shaw 15

1. Bill, a Police Officer, Is Raised Up from a Deathbed.................17
2. Gangrene Is Healed 26
3. God Hears Bella's Lament 29
4. A Desperate Young Lady Finds a Suitable Apartment.............33
5. A Man Is Spared the Amputation of His Hands........................35
6. A Lady Is Healed of a Broken Foot......................................39
7. Karen Is Saved from Suicide...42
8. My Neighbour Robert Is Healed of a Serious Flu...................46
9. Andrew, the Alcoholic, Is Delivered....................................48
10. Sheilla Is Healed of High Blood Pressure and Insomnia 52
11. Maria Feels Emotion 55
12. Peace Comes to Luke and Berta's House.............................59
13. Kim Finds Jesus and Lisa Finds Love for Her Father...............64
14. I Am Healed of a Detached Retina.....................................69
15. Vera Experiences a Victorious Passing 76
16. Julien Is Healed of a Brain Tumour....................................80
17. Miguel Experiences Divine Intervention While on a Secret
    Mission to Communist Russia 85
18. Sophie Is Able to Write Her University Exam.......................90
19. A Hit Victim Is Comforted..92
20. Carol Receives a Successful Kidney Transplant and a
    Troubled Traveller Is Encouraged....................................94
21. The Town Had Said "No," But God Says "Yes" 99

22. A Physician's Dire Verdict Is Reversed......................................100
23. A Woman Is Saved..107
24. Dinah Is Saved from Insanity...110
25. Fingers Are Restored To Normal Function............................114
26. Kendra Is Relieved of Pain..116
27. Alina Goes Back Home...117
28. Helena, a Polish Immigrant Doctor Receives a Miracle 124
29. Gerri Is Healed of a Brain Tumour.....................................127
30. Randy Is Miraculously Comforted in His Loss......................130
31. The Miracle Girl Survives a Serious Crash...........................132
32. A Baby Is Comforted..136
33. Sam Gets a Well-Paying Job in London...............................138
34. Rika Is Healed of a Serious Wound....................................141
35. I Keep My Million-Dollar View..144
36. Sabrina Has Her Sight Restored...146
37. Rambo Is Healed of a Bleeding Wart..................................148
38. Ramesh Seeks the Right Wife..151
39. Lina's Mom Is Healed of Heart Arrhythmia.........................154
40. John Receives a Miracle for His Heart.................................156
41. Jessica Is Healed of Bone Cancer 158
42. Prayer Blesses Bonita's Art Show.......................................160
43. An Electric Meter Runs Backwards.....................................162
44. Pierre Walks Without His Crutches.....................................164
45. I Am Healed of Phlebitis...167
46. Mary Anne Receives God's Help with a Difficult Court Case.......169
47. A Crying Newborn Is Comforted..173
48. Freddi Is Healed of Torn Ligaments....................................175
49. Murillo Has a Prosperous Year in University.........................179
50. My Four Prayer Requests Are Answered in One Day.............183
51. Kari Is Saved in Time 188
52. An Accountant Sees God's Hand at Work............................192
53. God's Presence Is Felt in the Vienna Bakery.........................194
54. Anna Is Delivered from Alcoholism....................................196
55. Gene Is Healed from a Botched Surgery..............................201
    Your Opportunity...204

About the Author

Suzanne L'Abbé was born in 1928 in a farming community near Sherbrooke, Quebec, Canada. She was the oldest girl in a family of nine children, so at a very early age she had to work hard to help her parents. When she was seven, the family moved to northern Quebec. When she was twelve she went along as a cook with her father (who was a stone-mason) and five other men to an English district to build a church. This brought her schooling, short as it was, to an end. It was her first exposure to the English language.

At fifteen, Suzanne got a job working as a maid in a town ten miles from her parents. There she met a man who became her husband. He moved her away from her family to a town in Ontario. Right from the beginning, the man took whatever money she earned and barely left her enough to live on. Together they had six children and she had to work very hard to keep them clothed and fed. When the older children were able to care for the youngest ones, she went out and found work. She would work all night and then care for her two babies during the day. By this time, she refused to give her earnings to her husband, so he would disappear for months on end. She finally divorced him. However, more than twenty years later, she was able to lead him to the Lord before he died.

Miraculously, Suzanne managed to buy a new unfinished house in Pembroke, Ontario, and there she raised her children. Over the eleven years they spent in that house, they managed to completely finish and brick it. Then, in 1975 she sold the house and moved to Toronto, where she bought a coffee shop and began building up a clientele, which became like family to her.

In June of 1976 she had a vision of Jesus in the middle of the night. He told her: "Fear not, for I am here, and I love you." From that time on, she read her Bible every day and prayed, and God answered her prayers. Many people who came into her shop received much more than a cup of coffee! Many were healed, counselled and encouraged in their faith.

Although Suzanne eventually sold her shop, she continued to pray and believe for those she met. Through the years, she has had many prayer partners.

Suzanne took the training by correspondence to become an ordained minister with The United Christian Church and Ministry Association (Rev. Richard Hall and Donald Warren). She also became an End-Time Handmaiden with Gwen Shaw's ministry. She has an extensive library of Christian books and continues to feed her faith through books and conferences.

All of the stories in this book are true and have happened to Suzanne. Most of the names are fictitious. May you be encouraged as you read these stories of an everyday woman bringing the blessing of God to those around her.

About the Title

One day, when my collection of stories was close to becoming a book, I said, "Lord, I need a title for my book."

I heard back, "It's coming."

The next day I prayed again, and this time I heard, "Get into my boat."

I phoned one of my prayer partner ladies and told her what I had heard, and she said, "Suzanne, keep on praying. Maybe God will give you something else."

The following day I prayed, and I got the same thing: "Get into my boat." Then I saw a lake and a boat. The Lord was rowing it. He came and took my hand and helped me into the boat and led me to a seat. He had a wool blanket, and He put it on my knees and then wrapped it around my legs. Then he gave me a sandwich on a plate. After I had finished eating it, He gave me a piece of cake on a beautiful plate.

Then Jesus pulled a net into the boat. It was like a big ball full of fish. Next, He rowed the boat a bit further. Alongside the boat, there was a long net full of fish. He was pulling this net in also, and He said to me, "Draw all men unto me."

A few days later, I heard, "Let's go fishing!" In this way, the title of the book came to me from the Lord.

Endorsements

I have known Suzanne for over a decade, and she has been an inspiration to me, as she is to many others. Her child-like faith and holy boldness is very evident in her everyday life to all of us who know her. Suzanne is one of God's handmaidens who passionately loves Him with all of her heart and so desires that others will also come to the saving knowledge of Jesus Christ. As you read these faith-building testimonial stories, may you receive your miracle.

Thank you, Suzanne, for your love for Jesus and your obedience in fasting and praying so that the work of God's Kingdom is done here on earth as it is in heaven. The Lord has used you to bring breakthrough in my life, as He has in countless others because of your surrendered life. God bless you, Suzanne, for believing that all things are possible with God. It is an honour working in the Kingdom of God together with you.

Pastor Carol McLean
Jehovah Jireh Christian Ministries

I am honored to have been asked to write an endorsement to the book entitled *Get into My Boat; Lets Go Fishing* by Suzanne L'Abbe. I have had the pleasure of knowing Suzanne for over 30 years, and this book is a graphic description of her experiences and deep faith in God. This faith has allowed her to overcome impossible odds in her own life, to make it a success. The same faith has allowed her to transmit the healing powers of God to others and help them to overcome impossible disabilities and diseases. In this book, she reaches out to a world where such ideas are an anathema, to try and demonstrate the power of faith. She has written this book to provide a vision of hope which people lack in our materially dominated Western society.

Khursheed Jeejeebhoy, MBBS, PhD, FRCPC
Emeritus Professor of Medicine

Foreword by Gwen Shaw

Suzanne L'Abbe's wonderful book on testimonies and miracles is a "page-turner." When I picked it up to read I just could not put it down. In fact, I stayed awake most of the night reading it. It seemed every story was a little bit too short; I wanted to hear more about every detail in every story.

Suzanne did a wonderful job of showing us how God can do miracles through anybody in the most simple ways and under the most unusual circumstances. As she stood in her coffee shop, the Holy Ghost worked through her and gave her the words and the insight into people's hearts. It seems like a story that is almost too miraculous to be true. I believe that God has given our sister a gift of miracles, that is one of the gifts mentioned in 1 Corinthians 12:10.

This book certainly built up my faith to believe God for greater things. After reading it, I went around with my head in the clouds, believing God for greater things in my own life, things I had almost given up on. And, just as it built up my faith, it will build up your faith too. You will not only want to read it, but you will want to share this book with many others because I know it will be a blessing to the entire Body of Christ.

This is even a wonderful book for those who don't know Jesus as their personal Savior because it is a selection of stories and testimonies that are for real.

God gave us such a wonderful jewel from French Canada, and to know that she is an End-Time Handmaiden has just thrilled me. God, raise up thousands like her in Quebec!

God bless Suzanne for writing this book, and God bless you as you read it.

Gwen R. Shaw, Ph.D.
President and Founder
End-Time Handmaidens, Inc.

❦ 1 ❦

Bill, a Police Officer, Is Raised Up from a Deathbed

Early one Monday morning in 1978, just a week before Easter (and the fortieth day of my fast), two police officers came into my coffee shop, and I said to myself, "Lord, what are *they* doing here?" I had been there two years and had never had a police officer come in, even one walking that particular beat. I knew they would order coffee, but I knew that there was another, very different, reason for them being there.

They did order coffee and cake, but soon they began to ask questions, and soon I sensed that the Holy Spirit had brought these two officers into my shop.

One of them, named Marvin, sat there in great sorrow, with his head lowered and said very little. The other one, Officer Tom, did all the talking,

"You are from Vienna?" he asked.

"No," I told him, "the sign was on the shop when I bought it. I'm from Quebec."

Then other questions came: "You like Toronto more than Montreal?" "Do you like Queen Street?"

I replied "No" to both of these.

"Do you like this job?"

I said, "No, because the hours are so long."

"Why didn't you stay in Montreal?"

I said I had another job besides this one.

"How can you have another job?" Tom protested. "You told us a minute ago you work twelve hours a day, six days a week."

"Well, I do my other job at the same time as I do this one," I replied.

This caused raised eyebrows. "We're interested in two jobs that can be done at the same time and both pay," Tom said. "We like that: two jobs and two paycheques."

Then I told them, "I pray for people."

"You WHAT?" he asked.

I repeated, "I pray for people."

"You mean p.r.a.y.?"

"Yes!"

"A... and what does that do?"

"Well, some people come back and say, 'You can stop praying now. I got my answer, Thank you very much.' "

"So you pray for your relatives and your friends?"

"Yes, but I pray for anyone who asks for my prayers, anyone with a problem or a need."

"Does it cost anything?" he asked.

"Nothing," I answered. "I have never read in the Bible that Jesus charged someone for healing them."

"We know there is no God," Tom said, "we don't believe in prayer in that way, and we never go to church."

"Well, that's your choice," I said. "I know there *is* a God, and I *do* believe in prayer, so I go to church and give Him thanks for answering my prayers."

"You could not pray for anyone," I continued, "because you don't believe. But I can, because I do believe."

Tom was curious now: "So you will pray for anyone who asks?"

"Sure," I answered. "Distance means nothing to God. If they meet the requirements, I pray for them."

"Uh, oh!" Tom said, a snide smile on his face. "Here comes the catch. I mean, I knew there was a catch, so what's the catch?"

"There are two questions I have to ask," I said. "First, I have to know the name of the person. If I said to God, 'I am praying for the man that has the blue shirt on,' and the next day he has on a red shirt, and someone else has on a blue shirt, then I would be praying for someone else. You see?"

The officers agreed with that simple logic. "So what's the next question?"

"The next question is exactly *what* am I praying for? I must know the need of the person. Does he or she want to buy a house or a car? Get a degree? Get married? Move to another country? Need healing? etc."

"This is all you need?" he asked.

I said, "Yes."

Just then a tear rolled down Tom's cheek, and he began to speak about a colleague, an officer named Bill, well-liked by all, who had been severely injured. When his car rolled over seven times, the two officers seated in my shop at that very moment had rushed Bill to a hospital, where their worst fears had been confirmed. After examining him, the doctors said,"We don't think that Bill has one bone left that is not broken. He will not live three days. Go home and prepare for his funeral.

Tom kept repeating to me that Bill "was such a good man," and that "everyone on the force loved him."

I asked Tom if he would do me a favour, and he said he would if he could. I said he needed to stop speaking of Bill in the past tense. "Stop saying, 'He was,' " I said, and instead, start saying, 'He is.' "

"For all I know, he could be dead by now," Tom protested.

I said, "Then he will be revived, because I will pray for him, and he will be fine." I pointed my finger at him, almost touching his nose with it, and said, "You can stop crying now."

Later Tom told me, "The doctors are saying that even if Bill is 'unfortunate' enough to survive, he will be in hospital at least six months, his mind will never be right again, and he certainly will never walk again. He will never work, never drive a car, and will need someone to look after him twenty-four hours a day every day. He won't even be able to dress himself or feed himself." I assured them that he would be fine.

On Wednesday afternoon, two days later, the two officers were back in the Vienna Bakery. I was standing at the till when Tom leaned over and whispered that his friend was still alive. "I know," I said.

He said Bill had died twice.

"I know," I told him.

With this, he got upset and asked, "Well, how did you know that? Did you phone the hospital?"

I replied "no" and a further "no" when he asked if someone had come into the shop and told me. "How do you know then?" he asked through a few tears, while his partner remained silent as usual.

As they sat with a coffee and the same cake they had ordered the first day they came in, I explained to them that I had a vision and that is how I knew Bill had twice died and been revived.

In the first case, in my spirit I had a vision of the hospital room, the day before, Tuesday morning.

There was a patient in a bed and two nurses walked in, and one of them pulled the sheet up over the head of the patient in the bed. I knew that this was Bill, the man I was praying for. He had just died. 'But, Jesus,' I prayed, 'I don't care if Bill just died. I know he will be fine." I never doubted it for one second, and I kept on praying, as I worked in the coffee shop, 'Lord, raise him up.'

"Then an hour after that first vision, I received another. This time two nurses again walked into the room where Bill was, and they proceeded to pull the sheet off of his face. *Praise God*, I thought to myself, *they revived him,* But he had been dead for a full minute. I knew that, but I was also sure the Lord was not going to let him die.

"The next day, Wednesday morning, the nurses were again in his room at 7:45. They pulled the sheet all the way down to the floor and then pushed the bed down a long dark corridor. In my vision, I said, 'Oh, Lord, he died again.'

"In my heart I was praying, 'Lord, I don't care how dead he is. I don't care if he gets as stiff as a 2 X 4; the man will be fine. I told those two police officers he would be fine, and he will be. If they were taking him to the morgue, then they will just have to bring him back.'

And, with that, I had smacked my fist on the countertop several times and shouted, 'Praise the Lord! The man will be fine!"

A customer, just coming through the door of the shop, heard me and asked if I was talking to him. I said, "No, Sir, I was talking to myself."

"I hope you get an answer soon," he said.

"I will," I assured him.

That customer sat at the table nearest the door, a place people rarely sat, if any other seat was available, because the door swung open and smacked into the table every time a customer entered. And yet he was the only one in the shop at the moment.

He asked for a cup of coffee and drank it very quickly. Then he put money on the table, grabbed the door open and ran across the street.

"My God," I thought, "I must have scared him. I guess he's never heard someone pray out loud before." But when it's a matter of life and death, one must get serious.

I kept on praying as I worked. Then, four hours later, I had another vision of the nurses returning the patient to his room. He had died again for four minutes, but they had been able to revive him. I again shouted, "Praise God!" I knew he would be fine.

The doctors and nurses now worked on him with much apprehension. They kept shouting things like, "He's not going to make it!" "He would be better off not living in this condition!" and "There's no hope!" In the confusion they shouted at each other, "Can't you move?" "Do you have both feet in the same shoe?" "Faster!" In desperation they worked on Bill, hoping against hope. "Hand me another needle! Faster! Faster!"

Bill survived, but even after he had been a week in the hospital I was told the doctors were saying he would be there six more months at least. Then, just twelve days after the accident, I spoke to an officer parked in a cruiser in front of my business. I asked him if he knew about the officer who had been critically injured in the car crash.

He said, "Everyone on the force knows Bill."

I told him I was praying for his recovery and I wanted to know his condition. He replied that Bill had already gone home. I nearly fell on my back right there on the sidewalk. I was shocked, not able to believe what I was hearing.

The officer said, "His mind is not right, and he doesn't want any visitors."

Maybe we forgot to pray for his mind, I thought. *We were too busy praying for his bones.* Anyway, I hadn't wanted to visit him. I didn't even know the man. I asked the officer if an ambulance had taken him home, and he said that he had walked out of the hospital on his own, without the aid of crutches or a cane.

About four weeks later, I managed to speak with another officer, and he told me that Bill had had a physical the day before. The doctor told him to please not ask any questions about his recovery because he didn't have any answers."I have never seen or heard or even read of anything like this in the medical journals, and I am an old man and have read a lot. If I had not known you before, I would never have believed that you are doing so well. You may go back to work on Monday. A little exercise certainly wouldn't hurt you, but otherwise there's not a thing wrong with you." The Monday when Bill went back to work was exactly six weeks after the accident.

In July of that year, Officer Tom came to see me and explained that he and Marvin had been transferred to another district. "Seeing how well your prayers worked for my friend, would you pray for my wife, myself and little girl. We're having marital problems."

I said,"I will."

Later, in the fall, Marvin came in one evening and asked if I remembered him. I told him I did. He said, "I hope you're still praying for us."

"I am," I assured him.

Decades have now passed, and I am still praying, not only for the two of them, but also for every officer on the force in my city.

≈ 2 ≈

Gangrene Is Healed

In the spring of 1979, late one Saturday afternoon a friend telephoned me and asked if I would come and pray for her. She said she had a severe pain in her chest, although she had been to visit her doctor earlier in the week, and he had said her heart was fine. I assured her I would be there shortly, and when I arrived she was still in pain. I proceeded to pray immediately.

The pain faded in a few moments, and she offered me a cup of tea, and we chatted for a while. She said, "I feel better. Stay a little longer. My husband Bob will be home soon. I'll ask him to walk you home. It's not safe for you to walk alone in the dark."

The husband arrived and was happy to walk me home. He had lived long in the area and as we walked, he talked about the neighbours, who they were and where they worked.

When we reached my place, I shook hands with him and said, "How is your leg?"

"Oh, not good," he replied, "but one must go to work. I can't stay home doing nothing. I have bills to pay."

I said, "I will pray for you, and your leg will be fine."

He wished me good-night and left.

The man was an alcoholic, and he had gangrene in his leg. He bandaged it every morning. His wife was avoiding him at the moment because of the smell of rotten flesh in the lower half of his leg. There was a hole about an inch across, and it leaked all the time.

His daughter, who was a nurse, had come to visit a few days prior and had said to her father, "I hope you realize you will have your leg amputated." The morning after he walked me home, he was changing his bandage, and he suddenly called to his wife, "Anna, come here! Come and see! My leg is better."

Skeptical, to herself, Anna thought, *Why should I go see? He has lied to me every day for the past fifty years.*" Finally, Bob left and went to work.

In the evening the man arrived home late, and as usual, he was drunk. The next morning he got up and proceeded to change his bandage again. But he didn't have to, because his leg was healed. He called Anna again, but she refused, so he went to work and in the evening he came home late again because he stopped at the beer parlour. The next morning, he again called Anna, and she thought that if she didn't go he would just go on calling like this forever. So she went and looked at his leg and was shocked by what she saw. Putting on her coat, she ran to my place and told me the leg was totally healed.

In the afternoon they both came back. The man showed me his leg, and there was no more hole. A brand new baby skin, soft and shining, had formed over it. Praise God!

～ 3 ～

God Hears Bella's Lament

She was an unassuming woman, but she now stood erect in the open doorway, as calm, cool and collected as a general in Adolf Hitler's army. Resting her left arm on the frame of the open door, she waited for him to leave.

He backed the car out of the garage and closed the garage door. Then he reached for the inside pocket of his jacket and pulled out his comb. Looking at himself in the rear-view mirror, he combed his hair one more time, then put the comb back in his pocket and straightened his necktie. He was very meticulous. He was wearing his best suit, of course, and a white shirt she had ironed perfectly. Even with the aid of a microscope it would have been impossible to find a crease in it. He looked like a prince and gave the impression of being Prince Charles' first cousin.

It was Saturday afternoon. He would not be home for supper again. It had become a ritual every Saturday for the past several months. Her blood was boiling in her veins. Nevertheless, she said not a word and neither had he.

Finally, he backed the car onto the street. She held her breath. He changed gears and floored the gas pedal, and we could smell the rubber burning. Without batting an eyelash, she pronounced the dreadful three-word sentence, and her urgent request thundered in the heavens: "God, stop Him!" even as he raced toward la femme fatal.

She closed the door, and as she walked to the kitchen, she remembered the promises of God's Word, "The prayer of a righteous man [or woman] has great power in its effects" (James 5:16, RSV). She was muttering to herself, "God will avenge me!" And her answer was to come *rapido*.

She took a plate, put some food on it and sat at the table, but never took a bite. For her, it was a dark day, indeed. They had married toward the end of the Great Depression. They were so in love that the Depression did not seem to matter. But as the years went by the family kept getting bigger with beautiful children (starving, naked, barefoot, penniless, as most people were at the time).

Then the war started, and the depression came to an end. Finally, there was food every day. He encouraged his wife, "When the children are all married and gone, we will have a good time together." She was waiting for that day to come.

Now as she sat in front of her plate of food, she became oblivious of the passage of time. The phone rang. A strange male voice at the end of the other end of the line said, "This is Officer Jerome. I would like to speak to Madame Belair, please."

"This is Madame Belair," she answered.

"I am sorry to inform you," he continued, "that your husband was in a car crash. We have finally managed to pull him out of the wreck, and he will be loaded into the ambulance momentarily. So far, he is doing as well as can be expected. We are taking him to Saint Justine Hospital. If you have no one to take you to the hospital, I would be happy to send one of our officers to take you there. The accident happened just about a mile from your home."

"Oh, thank you, Officer," she told him, "but one of my sons will take me."

Even as she said this, she was pondering in her heart, "If I had left the door open, I would probably have heard the crash."

She phoned the children and told them what had happened. One of the daughters said, "Mom, I am coming now. I will be there soon."

In the meantime, she was reflecting to herself, "How seriously is he injured? Will he walk again?

How long will he be in the hospital? Will he even live?"

The daughter arrived, and they went to the hospital and sat there and waited for hours and hours. For the next three months, there were many more trips to the hospital. Then he was able to go home. He had steel pins in his foot, his leg and his hip, and it was very painful. At the end of one year, he was able to go back to work.

He never again went out by himself, leaving her home alone, after these many years. He had learned a costly lesson. God had answered her prayers. Thank You, Jesus!

⮑ 4 ⮐

A Desperate Young Lady Finds a Suitable Apartment

A young lady came into my coffee shop late one afternoon and said to her friend, who was there already, "I am so sick of Toronto!"

The other girl looked surprised and asked, "Why?"

"I've been looking for an apartment for two years now," she replied, "and have found nothing. Every day, when the newspaper comes out, I am there to get a copy. I phone every place listed in the classifieds, and I get the same answer every time: 'Sorry, it's been rented,' or 'Sorry, it's already gone.' I am forced to live with friends, so I stay a month here and a month there, and all of my friends have to put up with me. I am sick of it, and they must be too. I'm sure of it."

I couldn't help but overhear the conversation, and at this point, I spoke up and said, "I will pray for you." At that, the lady began laughing, almost uncontrollably.

When she finally stopped laughing, she said, "I suppose you're wondering why I laughed?"

I said, "Yes, I was asking myself that question."

She replied, "I laugh because you said you will pray, and now I know I will find the place I need. When I was attending university, my landlady would say to me, 'Tell me when it's exam time, and I'll pray.' I would tell her, and she would pray, and I would get excellent marks on all my exams, even on the subjects I never had time to review. I never could understand that, but I now rejoice about it. Now you say you'll pray, so I know I'll find a place to live. So I'm very happy."

One week later, early in the evening, the phone rang, and it was she. "Hello," she said, "you don't know me, but I was in your shop last week, and I wanted to call and thank you because I found an apartment. I know you prayed.

"This apartment is in a better district than I had expected, the rent is less than I had anticipated I would have to pay, and it's more spacious than what I was hoping for. So, thank you very much for praying for me."

Thanks be to God!

⁓ 5 ⁓

A Man Is Spared the Amputation of His Hands

In January of 1979 one of my regular customers walked into my shop, and one glimpse at his face told me that he was in horrible pain. With great difficulty, he managed to remove his mitts.

When I had finished with another customer, I went to him. I looked at his hands, I felt I knew what had happened. I said, "You got drunk and fell down outside in the snow and then you fell asleep out in the cold and both your hands froze."

His answer was "Right on!"

The ends of his fingers were black, his fingers were purple, and his hands were dark red. The hands and fingers were very swollen and ice cold, and he could not bend them at all.

I had known this man for years, and I knew that he was an alcoholic. In the wintertime, he would frequently wet his clothes and come into the shop to get warmed up. He was very small and most polite. He always paid his bill and never broke anything (like most other alcoholics do). I really liked him. He was very nice.

The night he froze his hands was Christmas Eve, 1978, and it was recorded to have been the coldest night in a hundred years. When the police found him, while doing their rounds, his hands were as white as snow. They took him to hospital, where he had remained for five weeks.

"What did the doctor say?" I asked him.

"The doctor said I will have to have all of my fingers amputated. I have tried everything possible. I have contacted several other doctors, some even in different countries, and asked if they had any suggestions for my dilemma. But everything they mentioned I've already tried. I've come to the conclusion that there is no hope. I must resign myself to amputation."

I asked him, "Do you believe that Jesus could heal you?"

"Oh, I believe that all right," he said. I was rather shocked that he had answered in the affirmative.

"We could pray right now and ask Jesus to heal you," I said.

He said he would appreciate that a lot.

I got a little close to him and gently laid my hands

on his ice-cold hands. I had just started to pray,
when a man named John walked in shouting, "I need
two roast beef sandwiches to go, and I'm in a hurry.
Can I get that real fast?"

I said, " Yes, coming right up."

To the other gentleman, I said, "Hold on! I will be
right back, and I will pray for you." But, sadly, he got
up and left while I was making the sandwiches. He
later told me that he had been in so much pain that
he went home, took a pain pill and went to bed. (He
had a room in one of his brothers' homes.)

I was disappointed and said, "Jesus, he left, and
I didn't pray." In my spirit I heard, "I am the Healer,
not you."

In the morning, when the man got up he noticed
that opening and closing his hands was no longer
painful. He shouted, "I can't believe it! I am healed
and well! I can't believe it!"

He went to the doctor, as he had been doing every
morning. The doctor asked him what he had done.
"Nothing," said my friend.

"Don't lie to me," the doctor said, "I'm your doctor, and I have to know what you did."

"Well, I went to see this lady friend of mine, and
she asked me if I believed that Jesus could heal me. I
answered 'Yes, I believe that all right.' She said, 'We
could pray together right now and ask Jesus to heal
you.' I said I would appreciate that a lot. She started

to pray, but then she got busy. I left and went home and took a pain pill and went to bed. This morning, when I got up, there was no more pain. I was well."

The doctor then asked, "Is she a witch?"

"Whether she's a witch or not, that I don't know," the man answered, "but there's one thing I do know. Yesterday morning you said you would have to amputate all my fingers. Today you say I am completely recovered and well. That's all I care about."

Thanks be to God!

❦ 6 ❦

A Lady Is Healed
of a Broken Foot

A couple I knew owned and operated a store just up the street from my shop. Every summer they would take a month off to vacation at their cottage, as they did in the summer of 1979. It was almost dark when they arrived, and it was raining, but they were happy to be there. They lit the stove, prepared supper and ate. Then the lady went outside, and when she did, she slipped and fell and broke her foot.

X-rays revealed the foot was broken in three places. Surgery followed, and eventually she was walking again, but with two canes. Every day at 6 A.M. she had to go to the hospital for physiotherapy. When her husband came to the shop for coffee, I would say to him, "If you bring your wife over, I will pray over her foot."

He went home and said to his wife, "I don't ever want to see you in Suzanne's shop."

The next time he came in for coffee, he said, "I will pray instead of pay; all right?" He was making a joke of my prayers. But that did little for his wife, because x-rays showed the small break was getting better but the big one was not healing at all.

After six months, little had changed. It was now a few days before Christmas, and she wanted to go to the store and buy gifts for her daughters, but her husband wasn't helping much, and the sidewalks were icy. Walking with her canes in those conditions was simply too difficult.

One day she hobbled down to my shop, only to find the door locked. She had forgotten that I was closed that day. But I was upstairs and came down to get something, and when I saw her in the doorway I went over to talk to her.

"I'm sorry," she said. "I didn't mean to disturb you."

I asked if her husband had brought her over.

"No," she said, "he told me never to come here."

"Well, come on in, now that you're here," I said. I'll pray over your foot."

She warned, "My foot will smell."

"Who cares," I said.

I took her boot off and gently put my hand on each side of her foot and prayed. Then I put her boot back on.

"I had better hurry," she said. She got up from the chair and put on her coat and buttoned it. As she was putting on her mitts, she realized she was standing on her foot, and it was not hurting. She found that she could walk without the canes. So she put the two canes under her arm and went to the store and then back home.

The next morning she went to physiotherapy as usual, except she said "no" this time to the wheelchair. For six months, she had used it every day to get to her treatment. "You have needed it every day for the past six months. And today you don't need it?" asked a male nurse.

She walked past him, got on the elevator and rode up to the seventh floor. When her doctor saw her, he shouted, "Sit down! I told you not to put your foot on the floor." He was upset with her and decided on another x-ray, even though he had just done one three days ago. To his amazement, there was a big change. The two parts of the broken bone had now joined and started to heal.

The doctor was absolutely stunned by this. He didn't know what to say. And the lady could not say anything because her husband had told her never to come to my shop. So she could not tell anyone that she had come to my shop and that I had prayed over her foot. But she was extremely happy that she could now walk without canes.

Thank God for answering my prayers.

⪗ 7 ⪘

Karen Is Saved from Suicide

Even though I had never met Karen, we had become good friends. She was telephoning the church quite often for prayer, and I was a volunteer there. When her children got sick, I would pray with her. In time, we also exchanged home telephone numbers, so we could talk on weekends.

Karen had become a very needy person because of many bills she could no longer pay. Somehow she had lost her job, and her credit cards had been filled to the limit. She said to me, "My place looks like a palace; you should see it. Anything that makes the place look beautiful, I have it, but it is all charged on my cards, and now I don't have a job, so I can't pay. The creditors are phoning every day, telling me they are coming over to get a deposit on my account."

"My husband is shouting at me, 'Go to work and pay your bills!' but I can't find a job. Every time the mailman comes, he has another armful of bills.

"I bet you are not like that, Suzanne," she said. "In my mind I see your place. You have only the barest necessities. If you invite people over and one more person comes, you turn a crate upside down for that person to sit on. But you don't have bills coming in that prevent you from sleeping at night. Tell me if I am right."

"Yes, you're right on," I replied.

"In other words, you have peace day and night, and you don't jump every time the phone rings or the door bell chimes."

She also told me her children were very rebellious. "They're at the age of rebellion. They come home late from school, and if I ask a question, they mock me. If I ask them to do something, they say, 'Do it yourself!' I don't know what to do anymore. I cry a lot. Then, if they see me crying, they laugh. I don't understand why they're so abusive and hateful. I blame myself, Suzanne. Would you pray?"

"Of course! We can pray right now," I answered. So we prayed, and she was very thankful.

I did not hear from Karen for a while. Then one day, for no apparent reason at all, I called her early in the morning, before 8 A.M. I thought to myself, *It's too early! What is wrong with me?* But she answered, and her voice sounded horrible.

I said, "Karen, what is wrong with you?"

Her reply was, "I'm depressed. Could you call back in ten minutes? The children will have gone to school by then."

A few minutes later, I called again and asked her if she was sick.

"That's what the children are asking me," she said. "They're not mocking me anymore. They say, 'Excuse me,' if they have to walk in front of me. They're very quiet now, and there is no more laughter in the house."

"What are you doing today?" I inquired.

"I'm counting my pills. I never count my pills."

"What are you counting your pills for?"

"To see if I have enough. If I do, I'm going to commit suicide."

"No you are not," I insisted.

"Yes I am."

"Why, because you owe so much money?"

"Yes" she replied.

"So, after that your children will have no mother, your husband will have no wife, and you will have to be buried. Your husband will not throw your body in the lake. Funerals are costly. Every inch of the way, things would be much worse than they are now—financially and otherwise.

"Karen, put your trust in the Lord Jesus. He said, '*I will never fail you nor forsake you,*' (Hebrews 13:5, NKJV). Everything looks like hell on earth right now, but you will get better. You will find a job, and your bills will be paid. Most of all, there will be peace and joy in your family again.

"You can phone me any time of the day or night—you know that—and I will pray with you."

I called her several times that day. It was a fierce battle for her, but at five o'clock in the afternoon her peace of mind returned. She had come frightfully close to suicide, but I believe God prevented her from carrying out her plan to the end. Thank God!

⌘ 8 ⌘

My Neighbour Richard Is Healed of a Serious Flu

One night at 11 o'clock I decided to put my garbage out. My apartment has an inside chute, and as I entered the hallway, the resident next door was just arriving home. "Suzanne," he said, "don't come near me because if you catch what I have you will surely die." I knew he had been sick because I had heard him coughing day and night.

He said he had just come from the emergency department at the hospital, was there four hours and was running a temperature of 106°. "The doctors gave me some new antibiotics and said I have a bad flu."

He went back inside his apartment, and I went back to mine, but I got out a get-well card and wrote on it for him, "I will pray for you, and you will be fine." I pushed it under his door, and he picked it up and read it before going to bed that night.

Through the night, I did not hear Richard coughing as before and thought he must be feeling better. Then, in the morning, I heard water running in his kitchen sink and knew he was up. And he was still not coughing.

I was never able to talk to him about it until several months later. I was going out the front door one day, and I met Richard coming in. He shouted to me, "Suzanne, it works!"

"What works?" I asked.

"Your prayers," he said. "That next morning after you gave me the get-well card I got up, and I was fine, as though I had never even been sick."

Thank God!

~ 9 ~

Andrew, the Alcoholic, Is Delivered

One morning my landlord announced that he had sold the house where I had been renting a room from him, and I had one month to find another place to live. Since there was a shortage of places to rent in Toronto at the time, one could not be very choosy. I knew that if I found a place, I should take it, whether I liked it or not.

A short time later, I met some people who said they could rent me their living room, but I would have to share the kitchen and washroom with them. "You would have to put your food in our fridge and use our stove, but your room would be across the hall, totally separate from where we are, and you would have the key to lock the door," I was told.

So I took the place and soon learned that the couple had been living in the park and sleeping on the benches before they got their new accommodations, and they were not man and wife, as they had represented themselves.

They both worked part time. She slept in the bedroom, and the man, Andrew, slept on the kitchen floor, usually under the table. That beat the park benches and sewage grills where they had spent many cold nights. At least it kept her from freezing to death.

They put their money together to pay the rent, but their phone had been disconnected for lack of finances. So they made arrangements with me to use my phone, and that worked out fine for all concerned. They paid their share of the phone bill every month and never made long-distance calls. I was just thankful that I had found a place to stay.

When I went into the kitchen, I was shocked to find that there was plenty of space in the refrigerator for everything I had. All it contained was a half gallon of wine, three slices of bread, a little peanut butter and a glass of milk. *They have nothing to eat*, I thought. "Lord, I prayed, "surely today is payday, and they will bring some food home after work." But every time I saw Andrew he had a cigarette in one hand and a glass of wine in the other.

As much as I could, I tried not to infringe upon their privacy, but on the weekend I would run into them. All day Saturday and Sunday they stayed at home.

On Fridays, Andrew would bring home more wine and would drink more than on other days because he didn't have to work for the next two days. On Sunday, the lady would do the laundry and make supper and about 3 P.M. attempt to wake up Andrew for the evening meal. He would be sound asleep on the floor.

One Sunday when I came in, she told me that she couldn't get Andrew to wake up, and asked if I had any suggestions? I said she could try the water hose she was using to fill the washing machine.

"Yes, that would probably work," was her reply.

Some Sundays it was eight in the evening before he got up. But we all got along well together.

One particular day I walked into the kitchen and immediately noticed that something was different. Andrew didn't have his usual wine glass in one hand and cigarette in the other. I took an apple from the refrigerator and returned to my room with a question hanging in my mind about this change.

A few days later Andrew came to me to pay his telephone bill, and as he stood in the doorway of my room, he said he had something else to tell me. "One day, out of the blue," he said, he had stopped drinking, and then he added that three days later he had also quit smoking.

I was shocked and could hardly believe my ears, but I rejoiced in the Lord.

Andrew attributed the change in his life to my presence in his home and also to the prayers of his parents. Even though he had not asked me to pray for him, he sensed that I had been doing it.

I say, "Thank You" to Jesus and "Glory to God!"

❧ 10 ❧

Sheilla Is Healed of High Blood Pressure and Insomnia

In November of 2002 I travelled to the International School of Ministry near Jasper, Arkansas. The school is operated by Dr. Gwen Shaw, who is the founder and president. Along with Dr. Shaw, were four other professors to teach us, five periods each day.

One of the courses was on fasting, taught by Dr. Shaw, and I was excited about it because I knew of fasting as a child. My parents were Catholic, and they had to fast during the forty days of Lent. I used to help my mother in the kitchen, and I learned not to eat this and don't touch that, and don't put frosting on the cake. When Dr. Shaw completed her lesson, she asked for examples from the class about what happened when we fasted.

One man said he fasted for one day and "got a job" he wanted. Another fasted for three days and managed to buy a vehicle he needed. I then got up and said that on the fortieth day of my fast I prayed for a man that died twice and the Lord revived him.

That same evening, before the meeting started, a lady named Sheilla rose and asked a Dr. Robert Doorn to pray for her. She said she was very troubled with high blood pressure.

He said to her, "Turn around and look to the back of the room. Do you see a lady with white hair sitting there?" He was referring to me.

She said, "Yes," and he said, "Go and see her— her name is Suzanne—ask her to pray for you." So she came and sat in the chair next to me and asked me to pray for her.

She told me about her high blood pressure, and I said, "I will pray," but then I fell on top of her. "I'm sorry," I said, "I didn't mean to fall on you." My first thought was that someone had pushed me, an angel maybe. I didn't just fall. Then I thought, *God has a purpose and a plan in this*.

I prayed for Sheilla, and soon she returned to her seat at the front of the auditorium. About 10 P.M. the class was finished for the day, and we all returned to our rooms. The next day, before 9 A.M., Sheilla came to see me, saying she wanted to thank me for praying for her.

I said she had already thanked me.

"Now," she replied. "I thank you because I'm healed."

I asked her if she had gone to the doctor sometime between our prayers and morning. "I don't need a doctor to tell me I'm healed," was her response.

"So, how do you know you are healed?" I asked.

"For the past thirty years," she told me, "I have not had one good night's sleep. Thirty years is a long time to toss and turn in bed, never getting any rest. But last night I went to bed, and I was asleep before my head hit the pillow. This morning I woke up at seven, and I feel as young and energetic as I did when I was sixteen. I assure you I don't need anyone to tell me I'm healed. I know I'm healed."

Glory to God!

॰ 11 ॰

Maria Feels Emotion

One day in 1983 I was asked by my pastor to visit and pray for a lady named Maria in a nursing home. I agreed, even though he warned me not to expect any sign of appreciation, love, care or understanding from the woman. It seemed that Maria had no feelings or emotions, and this was the reason she had been incarcerated for some twenty-five years and had been in many different types of institutions. She was left alone, almost like a murderer, in what amounted to a life sentence.

Who sent her there? I wondered. *Was it her husband?* I doubted it. *Was it her mother-in-law, or another female? Who knows?* I was told the reason she had been sent there was that she didn't have enough love for her children. If that was the case and that was the proscribed treatment, many young mothers I knew could have been referred to this institution as well. I failed to see this as a proper solution.

It was my first time in this institution, so I stopped at the front desk and got the room number I should go to. When I arrived at the room, no one was there. Then I saw a lady coming up the hall, and when she got closer, I asked, "Maria?"

"Yes," said the woman.

"I am Suzanne," I said. "Last Sunday at our church one of your daughters requested prayer for you, so they sent me here to pray. Could I pray a little bit for you?"

She answered bluntly, "No! I have to go to bed now. The doctor said I need to rest."

"Maria," I said, "is it possible the devil is telling you a little lie right now?"

"Yes," she answered. "Why don't you just sit here beside me on my bed. Would you like to see some pictures?"

The first photo she showed me was of three beautiful young women. She said it was her and her sisters. "Can you guess which one is me?" she asked.

I said, "No, you all look alike."

"Well, take a guess," she said.

So I picked the middle one, and she said she was the one on the left. "You are so beautiful in this picture," I said.

"Well, this is when I was young," she said.

I had thought she was going to show me pictures of her children, but maybe she didn't have any.

She said she wanted to talk now and proceeded to tell me that she had six children. I told her I did too.

"Are they all living with your husband?" I asked.

"No, she said, "except for one who has not yet finished school, they're all married and living in their own homes."

Then I said, "I will pray for you now if you like."

"Yes, that's fine," she said. So I began to pray.

After a while, I started to weep. When the Spirit of the Lord comes upon me, this sometimes happens. She put her left arm around my shoulder and held me tight. With her right hand, she wiped the tears from my face, then dried her hands on her dress. As long as there were tears running down my face, she kept on doing this.

To say the least, I was shocked. This was the lady that was supposed to have no love for her family, but I could only see her actions as pure, unadulterated child-like love. This was the first time in my life I had been the object of such love (even counting my time as a young married woman), and it was coming from a total stranger, a woman deemed incapable of love.

I remember a day when I was crying when my husband came home. He said, "Go ahead and cry all you want. It doesn't cost anything." He did not bother to ask what was wrong or why I was crying. Comparing that attitude to Maria, I would say she had lots of love.

I finished praying, and she was very happy and most thankful. She walked me to the door, and I then said, "I will keep praying for you." She thanked me again and I left.

That evening, at the church, I had a talk with Rose, the youngest of Maria's children. In her heart, Rose desperately wanted to get her mother out of that institution. She said to me, "Suzanne, please keep on praying for me and my mom." I said I would, and she said she had already started the necessary procedures. "It'll take a long time ... so much red tape, but I still have another year of school to do."

After Rose finished school, it took her two more years before she got her mother out of that institution. She then kept her in her apartment for a year and then helped her to function by herself, so that by another year, Maria was able to get into her own apartment. Rose was now at peace, and she gave thanks to God and then got married and started her own family.

I am still asking God to forgive all those who were involved in locking up that woman, willingly or unwillingly. I also pray that God, in His mercy, will erase from Maria's mind the twenty-five lost years of her life.

⌒ 12 ⌒

Peace Comes to
Luke and Berta's House

In 2004 I was invited to my son Luke's for Christmas. Before I left home I was talking to God, and said, "Lord, today is Christmas Day, and we are going to celebrate Your birth on earth, which is a miracle. So, Lord, I ask for a miracle of my own. I want to see a miracle happen in my son's house while I am there today."

When I arrived at Luke's home, his wife Berta was in the kitchen putting away some pastries she had made. "Mom," she said, "I did not make pie this year, because I always seem to make too much dessert."

"I'm sure you'll still have too much," I said.

She then stated that Christmas dinner wasn't planned until the next day. "We are going to have food in the family room downstairs. Is that okay with you?" she asked.

"Excellent," I said, and with that we all moved down to the family room, where a table was set with lots of food.

I looked at it and thought it was strange they had bought a cheesecake. I don't ever remember seeing a cheesecake in their home or even hearing the word cheesecake there.

We sat around the table and talked and ate. Then Berta left and came back with a blanket and lay on the couch. "If you are finished eating why don't you relax and go to bed," I said to her. "In the morning when you are up making coffee, I can come down, and we can talk."

"I don't want to leave you alone," she said.

"Luke is here," I said, "and I would feel better if you are resting in your bed." She agreed and soon headed off to bed.

Luke made a fresh pot of coffee. I asked him if he was going to have a piece of the cheesecake. "We don't have cheesecake," he said.

"What is this?" I asked, pointing to the pastry in question.

"That's lemon pie. Berta made it. She's a very good cook. You should have a piece." Now I was puzzled. I called it cheesecake, and he called it lemon pie.

The first thing Berta had said to me was that she had not made any pies for Christmas. Yet, she had made this, but it didn't look like a pie. It had a straight up crust which was crinkly and golden in colour and looked more like a flan crust. Berta's crusts, although they are always white and look like they have been hiding in the shade for six months, are still very tasty.

After all my confusion, I took a knife and, noticing that someone had already taken a piece, cut one for myself. Luke asked me to cut one for him, as well, and so we sat, enjoying the pastry together. The colour of the filling was excellent, but I kept thinking to myself, *Berta did not make this pie*. It was simply not the way she made pie.

At 6 A.M. I awoke to the aroma of coffee, so I went down to visit with Berta, always an early riser. As I walked into the kitchen, she said, "Mom, you are right on time for the coffee. I hope Luke didn't keep you up too late last night."

"No, after you left," I said, "we had a piece of pie and coffee and shortly afterward went to bed."

She turned to me with a strange look on her face and said, "I told you I didn't make pie this year."

"Yes I know," I said, "but we had lemon pie. Maybe Luke got it at the bakery." Then I started to look for the pie, going through all three refrigerators and even on the shelf in the cold garage, but I could not find it.

When the granddaughters arrived in the kitchen, still in their pyjamas, they asked what I was looking for. Their mom responded by saying, "Grandma is looking for a lemon pie."

They both laughed and said, "We don't have any lemon pie."

"Your dad and I ... , we both had a piece of lemon pie before we went to bed last night."

Then the youngest one said, "Grandma, I think you're losing it."

Minutes, later Luke came into the kitchen, and I asked him, "Where did you put the lemon pie we had last night?"

"What are you talking about?" he said. "We didn't have lemon pie."

So now everyone in the house was laughing, and I was puzzled. I know the natural mind doesn't understand the things of the Spirit. Nevertheless, every miracle has a purpose. "Lord," I prayed, "I fail to see the purpose of the lemon pie, even though it tasted better than any lemon pie I ever made. I know there is a reason for it, but what?"

That night we were to have our Christmas dinner. The turkey was in the oven and was starting to smell good. As the day progressed, everything fell into place. The young people were downstairs in the family room. Luke served us tea. Berta was beginning to relax after a busy day.

"Isn't it peaceful in here now?" she said.

I agreed, and Luke added, "I only hope it stays that way."

I reflected to myself how amazingly peaceful it was, because the two granddaughters would usually be fighting with each other. Every time they were in the house together, it was more like a war than an argument, and it had lasted for more than a decade. It was almost impossible to think that peace would ever come to that home. The parents had been stressed to the limit by it, to say the least.

My daughter and I, along with many other relatives and friends, had prayed for Luke's family, and we were believing for a miracle. Two days later they were all back to work, and I was on the bus heading home. As soon as I got into my house, I had a vision and I saw Berta and my two granddaughters in their home standing in the kitchen eating a piece of that lemon pie. Now all the pieces of my puzzle were fitting together, and I gave thanks to God.

Now and then I telephone Luke's house and ask, "Is it still peaceful in your house?" The response is, "So far, yes."

I hope it will stay that way. Four years have now passed, and they still have peace. I rejoice greatly, and every day I give thanks to God for peace in their home.

⌒ 13 ⌒

Kim Finds Jesus and Lisa Finds Love for Her Father

A lady came into my shop one day with her three daughters, wanting a birthday cake for her eldest, Lisa. They were celebrating her twentieth. The mother purchased a beautifully decorated cake with Lisa's name on it, and they left rejoicing and laughing.

A few days later, Lisa came back very depressed. I was not busy when she came in, and I asked her, "Are you ill?"

"I'm depressed," she said, "and I know you pray for people. I was wondering if you could pray for me."

I asked her what the problem was, and her response was, "I hate my father."

"Oh, that is too bad!" I said. "What has he done to you?"

"Nothing," she said. I was a bit shocked by this answer, but then I listened as she proceeded to explain.

She told me that she simply could not stand her father. When he walked into the house, she would go to her room, returning to the kitchen only after he had gone elsewhere. Sometimes she would stay in her room and not have supper.

I said, "Let's pray." So we sat there and prayed, and after a little while, she said she felt better and went home.

A week later she came back. She said, "Suzanne, I don't know what you have done to my father, but he is totally changed. He now speaks to my sisters and me, and I've just had the best week of my life."

I was thinking, *It is not what I have done to your father, Lisa, but much more, what God has done in you.*

She proceeded to tell me that her father offered to drive her and her eighteen-year-old sister to a high school dance and pick them up when they were ready to come home. "Suzanne, that is the first time in my life that my father offered to drive us anywhere."

However, there was a problem with her youngest sister. She was getting close to twelve years old and was chubby. She was also a real bully, especially with their mother. Every day she hit her mother and made her cry. The mother could be seen with bruises on her face, arms and legs, where she had been kicked or punched by this preteen.

Sometimes the girl would skip a day or two of fighting with her mother, then ask for money to go shopping. Thinking the youngster was getting better in her temperament, the mother would give her the money, and off she would go to the shopping centre. A few hours later the telephone would ring and a police officer would be on the line asking the mother to come and get the daughter. She had been picked up for shoplifting, with the money still in her pocket. This was more than the mother could take, and she sat and cried, while the daughter shed not a single tear.

A few days later Lisa came again and gave me a report on the youngest girl. She said her mother was very discouraged and didn't know what to do. Then she said to me that Billy Graham was coming to Toronto in two weeks for a crusade and that she had obtained four reservations and tickets. She wanted me to go, but when she told me it was for a Saturday afternoon I explained that I had to work. Instead, I told her she should ask her little sister to go with her.

"Don't tell her she *has* to go with you, let it be willingly. Then please return and tell me what happens."

Days later Lisa returned, saying, "When the evangelist asked everyone that wanted to be saved to put up their hand and repeat the prayer, Kim did not put up her hand or pray out loud." Later on, the evangelist asked everyone who had prayed the prayer of salvation to come to the front. He said they would pray more and be given a little book that would explain salvation. "Kim sat in her seat and never moved," said Lisa.

"Finally we went home, and I felt very defeated with Kim." But then the following week Lisa said she noticed that Kim was not swearing at her mom like she used to. I knew then that it was probably only a matter of time before she would be changed dramatically.

"A few days later Kim found a cat outside and brought him in and asked Mom if she could keep it. Mom said 'no' because we already have two cats, but Kim continued to plead.

"I found it very strange that my sister would keep on begging. In the past, she would have simply said, 'I'm keeping the cat.' This time she just kept asking until Mom said 'yes.'

"When we were alone, I asked Kim, 'Did you give your heart to the Lord when the evangelist gave the alter call?'

" 'Yes' she said.

" 'I didn't hear you,' I said.

" 'No, I said it to myself,' " she replied.

Lisa said she could not believe her ears. She wanted to explode but held her breath until Kim left the room.

Then she came running to my shop. "Suzanne," she said excitedly, "Kim did give her heart to the Lord at the crusade. There are no more wars in the house, and mom is happy every day."

Thank You, Lord!

∼ 14 ∼

I Am Healed of a
Detached Retina

One May morning in 1980 I awoke totally blind in my left eye. I said to myself, "My vision is gone, but I am going to get it back." I worked in my shop the whole day like that, wondering why this had happened, but I found no answer.

The following day a nurse came into my shop to get some muffins. When she asked how I was, I said, "Fine, if I could see with both eyes. She asked what the doctor had said, and I said I had not yet gone to the doctor.

"Are you out of your mind?" she said. "Lock the door and run to the Emergency Room. Don't get on the streetcar. Run! It will only take you five minutes to get there."

I thought, "Jesus! She gets excited, doesn't she?"

It was about 5 P.M. already, so I finished my work and went to the hospital about 9 P.M. that night. There two student doctors took turns looking in my eye, thinking they could determine what was wrong. But finally they said they didn't know and called a specialist.

The specialist arrived and proceeded to examine my eye. He asked me how long it took to get to the hospital because the other doctors had said I had been like this for two days. He then suggested he would have run immediately to the hospital if it were his eye.

"That's you, doctor," I said. "I was raised during the Depression, and if I told my mother I wasn't feeling well and wanted to lie down, she would put a hand on my forehead and say, 'You don't seem to have a fever. Get your work done, and when you've finished the dishes, then you can go to your room if you want.'"

"For the fifteen years I was married, if I ever suggested I was ill, my husband would say, 'You're fine; get your work done.'

"If you have been pushed to the point of believing you don't even exist, then you don't take care of yourself, and you never need anything, no matter what," I explained.

When he asked what prompted me to come to the hospital this day, I told him what the nurse had said when she came into my shop.

At 11 P.M. that night the doctor finally informed me I had a detached retina and required immediate surgery. "I'll call the surgeon now," he said, "and within an hour you'll be in the operating room. So you should go call your son and tell him what's happening." He also told me that if I had come to him when it first happened I would have had a 0 to 80 percent chance of regaining my sight in that eye. But because I waited for two days, he said my chances had been reduced to 0 to 30 percent."

"Don't worry doctor," I kept telling him. "The Word of God says the blind shall see. I am blind, but I will see."

"Yes, sure, right," he responded, and then went to call the surgeon, only to learn he had left for Boston and would not be returning until Sunday (and this was Friday night).

The doctor was not happy about this. Every hour that passed took us further away from success, he explained. When you have a detached retina, it must be reattached within hours, not days. This wait made him very sad.

I said it was fine that I would just go back home, and he could call me when he was ready. He looked at me sternly and said, "You will do no such thing! I have ordered a bed for you." He told me to go ahead and put on a gown and a nurse would come and roll me to my room as soon as one became available.

I woke up the next day on the seventh floor of that hospital and was told not to get out of bed. "Complete bed rest" was the doctor's order. So I stayed in bed all Saturday and Sunday and late that afternoon, Doctor Larry, the specialist, finally came to see me. The surgery was supposed to occur at 6 P.M. He looked in my eye and said the same thing all the other doctors had said: "If only you had come in sooner ..."

I said, "Don't worry, doctor, the Word of God says the blind shall see."

His reply was similar to all the others: "Yeah, right, sure."

I was later told the surgery would not be done that evening but at eight o'clock on Monday morning instead. It was Queen Victoria Day.

I was ready for surgery by 8 A.M. the next day, but, strangely, I didn't see Doctor Larry all day, and no other doctors came by to see me either.

Finally, at 6 P.M., two nurses came to my room to say that it was my turn for surgery. "We're taking you to the OR. I was thinking: *What happened to their old adage about every hour taking us further away from success?* In their minds, I supposed, I would be just as blind after surgery as I was right then, so there was no rush. It was already too late.

When he visited me on Sunday the surgeon had explained all that could happen with this type of surgery. He said I might lose the other eye and become totally blind. I could be in bed for six months, requiring someone to look after me twenty-four hours a day. I could be paralyzed and never be able to move again, or I could lose my mind and be placed in a mental institution. He said I might need several blood transfusions, and then he said there was something worse than all that put together.

At this point, I interjected, "There is something worse than all that put together?"

"Oh, yes," he said, "if you get an infection, then we are in BIG trouble!"

He also explained that even if everything went well, I would still have to visit him every morning in the hospital for two months. As he started off down the hall that day, I shouted after him, "Oh, doctor," I said, "God bless you!"

He stopped and said, "Thank you," and then disappeared, and I started talking to God.

"Jesus," I said, "You and I both know that I will not be coming here every morning for two months. I will be sick in bed and not well enough to get up to come here."

My church sent a couple to come and pray with me, and they arrived after the surgery. The woman said that she'd had an operation on her eye, and she had to come to see the doctor every day for two months and was in so much pain she could not take public transit, but needed to use a taxi. She lived twenty miles away, and it had cost her a fortune. I said to the Lord, "This will not be my portion."

As I was being wheeled into the operating room, there were two doctors, and they were debating about which one was going to dinner. One said he was getting the instruments ready and then leaving, and the second said he would put "the patient" to sleep, and then he was leaving. By the tone of their voices, I thought both would be leaving.

I was shifted onto a narrow cart, and the nurse strapped me down. Then I saw Jesus standing at my feet, and I said, "Jesus, don't leave me here alone." The next thing I knew I was in recovery and in pain.

At 11 P.M. I was wheeled back to my room, and my son Yvan and his wife Phyllis were there, but I suggested they go home. I was in pain and lamenting too much. I did not sleep that night.

Twelve hours later, Doctor Larry came to my room and said the surgery had been a success. He took the bandage off my eye and opened it with his fingers. Then he examined it closely with a light, moving from side to side. Even though my eye was full of blood, I could see every move he made.

I said nothing; I was still hurting too much, but I said in my heart, "Thanks, God, I can see."

Before the surgery I had been able to see absolutely nothing, but I remembered one of the doctors saying that if I got any vision back it would continue to improve through two years. "Of all the organs in your body, your eyes are the slowest to heal," he said. He was right. For the first year, things would appear small and distorted.

Six days after surgery, Dr. Larry came to see me. "I don't understand," he said, "I have never seen anyone heal so fast from eye surgery." He said I could go home the next day, and then I remembered his assertion that I would have to come and see him every day. "It will be fine if you can come every two weeks," he said.

I said, "Oh, thank You, Lord!"

Six weeks later I went for a vision test. I looked at a chart and then said, "Doctor, I will be a disappointment. All I can see are four little black dots."

He jumped about two feet off the floor, clapped his hands together and said, "That was great!"

I asked what was so great about it. "Are those dots not supposed to be letters?"

He said, "No! And they're not little dots either, but, great, you can see." Then he turned the roll, and the numbers grew larger, and I read them.

"Did I not tell you I was going to see?" I asked.

"You told us all right, but we certainly did not believe you," he admitted. He now went from one nurse to another, whispering to each, "She can see."

A year and a half later I had my eye tested again, and Dr. Larry declared my vision had reached 98 percent or better.

Thank you, doctor, and praise be to God.

~ **15** ~

Vera Experiences a Victorious Passing

Vera and her boyfriend Bob were from Romania. They came to Toronto separately and met in church. The following year their church put on an engagement party for them, as they had few local friends and no relatives.

At that engagement gathering, I had the opportunity to speak to Vera at length and was quite impressed. She sounded so nice that I fell in love with her right then and there. She had taken courses at the University of Toronto but still had no job interviews. I told her she was clever and intelligent, and she would soon be working, and life would become easier.

"Yes, I believe that," she said.

Vera loved the Lord with all her heart and trusted in God implicitly. In Romania, she had been married, but her husband was a cruel man, and she was finally able to get a divorce from him. She saved her money and eventually managed to come to Canada, wanting to put distance between her and her ex-husband.

In Toronto, she worked during the day and went to school in the evening, but her health was somewhat frail, and she was emotionally frail as well. At the same time, she was courageous in looking to the future and planning her wedding. The pastor of their church was helping them, and soon she and her fiancé would be married.

Vera was certain all would now be fine, but a few months later she had to go see a doctor. He kept calling her back for more tests and eventually diagnosed her with cancer. From then on, every time I saw her she looked more pale and withdrawn. To make matters worse, it turned out that her new husband was not healthy. He could not hold a job for more than a week, sometimes only a few days, and he did not help her with any of the household chores, making her life all the more difficult.

Now and then she would be admitted to the hospital for three weeks to a month at a time. No one would know, and we would only find out when she had returned home and gave us a call.

As the weeks passed, she was admitted to hospital once again, and this time the doctor told her husband she would not be going home anymore. Bob was in shock. His first wife had left him, and now Vera was dying.

It had never entered his mind that this might happen. He then began to call her friends, letting them know she was paralyzed from head to toe on her left side. She was being fed intravenously and could hardly utter a word. Her voice was but a whisper, and her eyes remained closed.

When I went to see Vera, I could hardly understand what she was trying to tell me. She was now totally paralyzed and unable to move even a finger. The doctors wondered how she was even still alive.

One day, while I was there visiting, a nurse came in and said Vera had a bit of a fever, so they wanted to give her a sponge bath. "Suzanne, put on these rubber gloves and help bathe her," she said. "You can do it as well as we can."

I did that, and the nurse left to get new sheets, and then we put fresh sheets on Vera's bed. It was now a matter of waiting for the inevitable.

No one else was coming to visit Vera anymore. I went at six each evening and stayed until nine in the morning, when her husband would arrive and stay for the day. It was wintertime, snowy and cold, and I found it difficult to get to the hospital.

The nurses were quite friendly, and one day one said that I should go with her. She took me to their kitchen, where there was a refrigerator stocked with lots of food, and I could even make a hot drink there. Then she took me to the linen cupboard and showed me pillows, sheets and blankets and told me to fix a bed for myself on the big chair beside Vera's bed.

I said, "I can't do that. I might fall asleep."

"Well, that was the idea," said the nurse. Instead, I stood beside Vera's bed and held her hand all night for two weeks.

Two days before Vera died she lifted her right hand up into the air, apparently defying her paralysis. She wrote three sentences, each one below the other. I was in shock and kept repeating, "Lord, what did she write? Lord, I want to know." But no matter how often I asked Jesus, He was silent, and I heard not a word until after the funeral.

Three days later I was sitting at my dining room table, ruminating on the events of recent days, when all of a sudden the Holy Spirit spoke and said, "She wrote, 'Jesus is coming soon! Jesus is coming soon! Jesus is coming soon!'" Glory to God!

❧ 16 ❧

Julien Is Healed of a Brain Tumour

One day my brother Léo phoned me from Ottawa, where he was working installing replacement windows in older buildings. He said his boss had just asked him to come to Toronto and change some windows at the University there. He had wished he could say no, but he felt he had no choice. This was to be his first visit to Toronto, and he was nervous about the size of the city and the traffic. Nevertheless, he said, he *was* coming.

The reason he was calling was to ask if he could bring a man by my place so that I could pray for him. Of course I said, "Yes," and he answered, "Then I'll see you on Monday."

When I hung up the phone, I was rather stunned. At that time, I had never told anyone in my family that I prayed for people. So how could my brother know? It was a mystery to me.

On Monday, he arrived with the man in question, someone named Julien. We talked for a while, and then Julien began telling me his problems. He was born deaf in his left ear and had undergone surgery as a very young child. He would often hemorrhage and then pass out, and each time this happened, his mother would send someone to the convent and ask the nuns to pray for him, and he would be revived.

He now suffered from severe headaches, which almost drove him insane. When he felt these headaches coming on, he would go home as fast as he could and then ask his wife not to turn on the television, not to boil water on the stove, not to put the cat out or even turn a page of a newspaper, but to just sit still and wait until it was over.

I said to him, "Now you are ready for prayer."

"Yes," he said,

I asked him to kneel down, because he was tall and I wanted to put my hands on his ears. He did this, and I prayed for a minute or two. Then I said to him, "That's all. You can stand now."

"That's all?" he asked. "I'm done?"

"Yes," I said.

He got up then and said, "I am healed."

I asked, "So you can hear now?"

"No," he said, "I still can't hear anything out of that ear."

"Then why," I asked, "are you saying you are healed?"

"Because I know I'm healed," he said. "When you put your hands on my ears, something twisted and turned in my head and then pulled out of my head. Everywhere your fingers were touching my face, it was burning like fire! So I know I'm healed."

"Well, don't be concerned," I assured him. "Perhaps within a few days you will hear too."

As soon as their work was finished in Toronto, the men returned to Ottawa, and the following day, Julien made a visit to his doctor. One of the first things the doctor asked for was his list or record of recent headaches.

"I don't have a list," Julien said, "because I haven't had any more headaches."

This didn't please the doctor, who said, "Now I specifically told you to keep an accurate account of the length and intensity of your headaches. And you didn't do it. As soon as you began feeling better, you forgot. Now we have nothing to go on because it's not possible that you didn't have a single headache. So don't try to tell me that. Go home and come back next week with your paper."

But the next week it was the same; Julien had not had a single headache, and therefore he didn't have a list for his doctor. The doctor kept protesting, "But that's not possible! Now, go home, and if by next week you still say you haven't had a single headache, then we'll do some more tests and x-rays.

Without Julien's knowledge, the doctor had told his wife and parents that he had a brain tumor and would not live to see his next birthday. He was just twenty-nine at the time. All Julien knew was that he had an ear problem that had been causing him headaches.

The following week, Julien again reported to his doctor that he had been free of headaches. The doctor said, "Then we'll do some more tests and x-rays, and when you come next week, we'll have the results. But when Julien went to his next appointment, the doctor said, "We're going to have to do more tests." He had not been able to find the tumor and wondered where it might be hiding. Again more tests were done, and Julien was told to come back the next week.

The following week, when Julien arrived at the doctor's office, he was asked to come in and sit down. "I have something to tell you," the doctor said. Julien took a seat. "Julien," the doctor said, "if you die today or the next day or even next week, it will not be because of the tumor you had on your brain, because it's gone and you are perfectly well."

A few months later, at ten-thirty one Sunday night, my phone rang, and a lady's voice asked, "Is this Suzanne?"

"Yes," I said

She said, "You don't know me. But do you remember in the summer when your brother came to see you? Well, the man named Julien who was with him was my husband, and you prayed for him. The doctor had warned me that he could drop dead any moment because he had a brain tumour. Now, that tumour is gone, and I just wanted to thank you for praying. We are so happy!"

Thank God!

❧ 17 ❧

Miguel Experiences Divine Intervention While on a Secret Mission to Communist Russia

Miguel lived in Israel with his wife and children, but from time to time he would come to Toronto, and I would see him in the Queensway Cathedral Church where I attended. He was a film producer.

Once Miguel came to Toronto and spoke to our prayer group and asked us to cover him and his associates with prayer every day for two months. He told us he was going into a Communist country, Russia, and if its police force, the KGB, discovered what he and his group were doing there they would shoot them, no questions asked.

He and his associates were only going to be inside of Russia for a few days of the two-month period, but he was not certain when that would happen, so I prayed every day of those two months, particularly in the evening, when my normal work was finished for the day.

One day I called a friend and asked if he would pray with me on the telephone. He agreed. I was in my bedroom/office on the second floor, and as we prayed I had a vision of three men dressed in black from the top of their heads to the soles of their feet. The vision was so real that I thought to myself, *How were these men able to get up the stairs and through two locked doors and into my office without me hearing anything?*

Then one of them drew a pistol and pointed it at me, and I shouted for him to drop the gun, in the name of Jesus. I shouted that for five minutes or more, and then very, very slowly he opened his hand, and the gun fell to the floor. One of the other men had a black handkerchief and kept blowing his nose into it. The vision was so real I was sure they were in my house. Then the vision disappeared.

Soon the thought came to me, *My God, my Israeli friends have been arrested.* In the vision I had seen the pistol dropped, so I believed they were still alive. Of that I felt sure.

They could not have been shot because of all the people in the world who were praying for them. It would have been impossible, God is faithful to hear us when we pray.

From then on, every day I was asking myself the question: are they in jail or did they go back home to

Israel? I wondered if I would ever know if they had been successful in their endeavour or not.

Then, two years later, one Sunday morning I saw Miguel sitting four rows ahead of me in church. I got his attention and asked him if we could talk after the service, and he agreed.

There were many others who wanted to speak with him too, and so I had to wait my turn. It came about two hours later.

I began to ask my questions, but he stopped me, almost as if in fear and asked, "Why are you asking me all these questions?"

I explained to him, "You asked us to pray for success on your mission to Russia. One evening I was praying for you on the phone with a friend."

"Oh, I see," he said. "Ask all the questions you want."

I told Miguel about the vision and asked him, "Did you get arrested?"

He confirmed, "We got picked up by the KGB while we were waiting to board our plane. They took us to the police station and questioned us for eight hours non-stop. They took pictures of us ... so many. They unrolled my film onto the floor and walked all over it with their big boots."

Miguel then said that, at the end of the interrogation, the police told him he could keep his film, but they seized all of his documents.

"I had been in England on a fund-raising tour," he said, "and I went to many churches. At one of those churches an elderly lady came up to me and said the Holy Spirit told her that I would be going on a secret mission soon. She said, 'Make sure you duplicate all your documents.' "

Miguel said he heeded the woman's advice and so later he was able to retrieve the duplicates of all the documents the Russian police had seized. "When they released us, we returned to the airport," he continued, "and boarded the airplane to the next country (where he had sent by post his copied documents). I went to the post office and there retrieved all the documents waiting for me and was able to return safely to Israel."

"Why did you go to Russia in the first place?" I asked.

"I went there to investigate how the Christians were being treated and see what I could do to help the Jews return to their homeland."

Miguel then told me that just prior to his arrival in Russia, a boy of sixteen had been beaten to a pulp and left on the sidewalk because he was a Christian and had requested a visa to visit Israel for two weeks.

"We were walking on pins and needles day and night, never knowing what would happen in the next moment," Miguel said. "I interviewed a lot of people and took many pictures, since I had many addresses and contacts." He said he was planning to help as many Jewish people get out of Russia as possible and make their journey to Israel.

Then came my question, "Miguel, what day was it when you were returning home?"

When I told him, he answered, "It was the last week of September, a Monday or Wednesday." Then he asked, "Why do you want to know?"

I said, "Because the last week of September on a Monday night is when I was praying for you on the phone with my friend, and that's when I had the vision of the men and their guns."

He gave me a big hug and said, "Sister, do you see how important it is to pray? If people would not have prayed for us, this story could have had a very tragic ending."

As it happened, after much planning and work, thousands of families were helped to rejoin their loved ones and get back to the country of their ancestors, where they have found hope, work, home, food, peace and God. Thank You, Lord, for people that dared.

~ 18 ~

Sophie Is Able to Write Her University Exam

It was exam time at the University of Toronto, and Sophie, a young music student there, had finally gone to the doctor after being home sick all week. He gave her a prescription, some pills to take with water daily, and told her to stay in bed until she felt better. She had bronchitis, and her throat felt like it was on fire. Her voice was a mere whisper, and she was burning up with a fever ranging from 104° to 106°.

Sophie was definitely sick, but more so, she was in a panic about the exams that were scheduled to start on Monday. "If I don't write these exams," she told me, when I went to visit her on Saturday evening, I'll have to repeat my year."

I asked her if she would like me to pray for her.

"I'm not much of a prayer person," she said, "but now I'll take everything that's offered."

I proceeded to say a short prayer, and just after I had said, "Amen!" Sophie immediately said, "I'm healed." Her voice was now loud and clear, and the burning in her throat was gone. I touched her and found that the fever was also gone. On Monday morning, she went to her class rejoicing and praising God.

~ 19 ~

A Hit Victim Is Comforted

It was a beautiful summer day, and I was on my way to the bank to pay my bills. The sidewalk was all but empty, and my thoughts were on a quick return home, because I had so much to do.

On my way back from the bank, I saw a crowd of people on the sidewalk where I had earlier passed, and I wondered what had happened in such a short span of time. As I approached, I was told that a person had been struck by a car. I pushed through the gawkers and saw a black woman lying on the pavement with her head up on the sidewalk. She was bleeding and moaning in pain. I knelt beside her, put my hand on hers and prayed, "May the peace of God be on you."

She immediately stopped her moaning. I was not sure if she could hear me when I told her, "An ambulance is on the way, and they will take care of you. I will keep on praying for you after I get home," but I thank God for taking away her pain and comforting her in that moment.

Glory to God!

❧ 20 ❧

Carol Receives a Successful Kidney Transplant and a Troubled Traveller Is Encouraged

I was on the bus going home to Toronto from Waterloo one day when a gentleman came and sat down next to me. I had made up my mind that I was not going to enter into any conversation on this trip. Instead, I was planning to just close my eyes and relax.

"It's a beautiful day," he said, and I responded that it certainly was. We exchanged other pleasantries and talked about various things, and the next thing I knew I was telling him the story of my younger son's mother-in-law, Carol.

As I did this, I was wondering why. *He is not interested in this, I am sure. What is wrong with me?* Nevertheless I kept on talking about it.

I told him that Carol is a specialty teacher working with mentally challenged students, eleven in all in her class. This might be considered a small class, but considering the mental health of these students, I am sure that by 4 P.M. every day Carol is worn out. But she loves these children and enjoys her work with them.

And that is just one part of Carol's difficult week. Both her kidneys have been burned out by radiation from cancer treatment, and she has to have dialysis every three days. She lives out in the country and is an hour drive from her work and almost the same distance from the hospital. Because of the fluid build-up, she is sick to her stomach and after each treatment she will drive home as sick as a dog and then not sleep very well, but still has to get ready for school the next morning. She arrives before the students at 9 a.m. each day, no matter how she feels. And she goes through these tribulations every three days.

I told him her name was on a list for a kidney transplant, and she has even been called twice and made the three-hour trip to the transplant hospital, only to be told the donor kidney had been unsuitable.

I then explained to my travelling companion that one day I just happened to turn on the television, a rare occurrence for me because I usually only use it to watch my videos. The 700 Club program was on that day, and a pastor had just finished praying, and then offered words of knowledge to the physical audience and those watching by television. He said, "Someone has a kidney being healed, or they will get a transplant." I immediately took that word for Carol. I was sure it was for her, but she lives in the United States. I prayed for her, believing she would soon get well.

About a month later, my son telephoned to say that he and his wife were leaving immediately for New York. It appeared that a suitable kidney had been located for Carol, and the transplant surgery was scheduled. They wanted to be there before she went into surgery (and, in fact, they got there in time). Best of all, six days later Carol was back home. This all happened in the mid-1980s, and Carol is still doing well twenty-five years later.

I had finished telling my bus traveller that story when we arrived at my drop, to catch the subway home. He shook hands with me, and said, "Thank you very much." Somewhat puzzled by that, I asked him what I had done to merit thanks. He said, "When I sat down with you, I was poor, miserable and wretched, with at least a thousand problems. Now that I have heard your story, I am the richest man in the world, and I am very happy and don't have one single problem. So, thank you." Now I understood why I had told him the story.

Praise You, Lord God Almighty!

∾ 21 ∾

The Town Had Said "No," But God Says "Yes"

One day I was invited to attend a church in the country about sixty miles away. One of my friends was going to drive there to hear some special guests coming from the United States for a three-day conference. We arrived just before the meeting started.

The church was very nice, but small, and did not have running water or washroom facilities —just a portable toilet outside. Surprisingly, it had been operating in that fashion for six years already. Every year they had put in an application to the town for a building permit to make updates but were always turned down.

I knew no one there, but after three days I felt comfortable among them. I was thinking, *These people are very friendly, and they are working very hard to bring this church to prosperity, not only financially but spiritually. They desperately need to put an extension on the building and to bring in running water.* When I returned home, I prayed and asked the Lord if there was anything *I* could do to help them get their building permit. The answer I received came in two groups of twelve days each of fasting. The Lord told me which day to start, so I did the first twelve days. Then I had to wait for three weeks, and the Lord then told me to start again for another twelve days.

When my fast was finished, I learned that Prophet Johnnie from Indiana had come to that church and prophesied that something in the spirit world had been blocking the approval of the building permit. Whatever the problem, it was now resolved.

A short time later the church got its building permit and added its extension, with washrooms and running water, and the congregation greatly rejoiced in the Lord with much thanksgiving. And I also give thanks to God!

~ 22 ~

A Physician's Dire Verdict Is Reversed

In 1984 I sold my coffee shop, where I had worked for twelve hours a day, six days a week, for nine years. I loved my customers and prayed for many of them, and I enjoyed my work.

After that, I had to find something else to do, so I started babysitting. One day I realized that in my phone book I had seven different addresses and phone numbers, three of them being my own sons'. The only thing these young couples had in common was that they all had young children.

Their needs for babysitting were all different. One said, "I would need you only on Saturday morning: we go to the market and then we have lunch before coming home." Another said, "I would need you once in a while on Friday night when we go to the movies."

Some would invite me for a meal at their home sometimes, so I had more than full-time work. For my sons, I worked the longest time.

One night I had a dream. In the dream, someone was having a baby, and I was trying to figure out who the parents were. I went up and down the line in my mind, but I could not think who was going to give birth to this baby.

The baby looked so horrible in the dream, more like a monster. All I could say was, "Oh, God, no! Oh, God, no!" and, "God, please erase this picture from my mind!" He did, and it never came back, but I couldn't stop thinking, *Who will take care of this baby?*

Then the thought came to me that this was not just a dream. We sometimes say, "Don't worry; it's just a dream." This, however, was a reality, and it would take place, whether I liked it or not. But who were the parents?

Then one day, I got a call from Kirk and Jalene saying, "Would you like to come for supper tonight?"

I said, "Yes, okay, that is very nice of you," but as I put the phone down I thought, *They have never invited me during the week, always on the weekend. This is very strange.* I couldn't figure it out.

I got to their place just before seven. The table was set; everything was ready. We sat at the table and started to eat. The food was excellent, as usual. Then Kirk announced that they were going to have a new baby.

I froze on the spot! I knew I should offer congratulations, but not a word would come out of my mouth.

I was in an absolute frenzy. I sat there, staring straight in front of me, not looking at either one of my hosts. All I could think of was the baby in the dream.

After what seemed like an eternity, I finally said, "That's nice."

I am sure both of them were saying to themselves, "What on earth hit her?"

I was thinking, *I don't want anybody that I know to give birth to this baby that I saw in my dream, not even my worst enemy—if I have one!*

Finally, Jalene got up and took our plates to the kitchen and came back with the tea and asked if we wanted pie and ice cream.

I said, "No, thank you." My mind was still in shock, but I knew I had to gather myself together and pretend everything was fine.

I then said, "I'd better go before it gets too dark outside." I left by the back door. But then I stopped behind the garage and prayed, "Lord, don't let me get hit by a car on my way home." My eyes were full of tears so that I couldn't see. My mind was still in turmoil, and I had lots of streets to cross to get home, but I made it safely, thanks to God.

I had been working for Kirk and Jalene for a few years, taking their children to school in the morning and getting them back home in the afternoon and looking after them till the parents got home. One month after they had told me they were going to have a new baby, I noticed that Jalene was seeing a doctor every Monday morning. (Because I worked there every day, I noticed what was taking place.) I thought that was not normal for the early stages of a pregnancy. Maybe in the last months it would have been more normal, but not now. So, I was wondering what was wrong. At the same time, I was thinking about my horrible dream of a deformed baby. But I dared not say a word.

Shortly thereafter, Kirk and Jalene came home one evening around six P.M., as usual. But they walked in with their heads down, looking at the floor. They said not a word. They looked as though they had come from the court house and a sentence of death had been passed on them. I knew something was very heavy on their hearts.

They went upstairs, changed their clothes and came back down. Then they started the supper. There was still no smile on their faces, and Kirk said they didn't need me any more that day.

I came back the next morning just before eight o'clock, and there was no change on their faces. I was thinking for sure it was the unborn baby that worried them. How could they go to work every day in that frame of mind? I was praying, but nothing was changing, or so it seemed.

A week or so later, I was at their house again. I took the children to school, then I came back to do some laundry. I carried the clean laundry up to their room, and there I noticed an opened letter on Jalene's dresser. I thought that was strange because in all the years I had worked for them I never saw an open letter in the home.

I wanted to leave the room, but the Spirit said to pick up the letter and read it. "No, Lord," I said. "It is not addressed to me, and therefore I cannot read it."

The Spirit said again, this time louder, "Pick the letter up and read it."

I said, "Lord, we do have a protocol. We do not read other people's mail." I am sure the Lord knew all of that before I said it. But, for the third time He said, more sternly this time, "Pick up this letter and read it!"

This time I said, "Yes, Sir!"

I saw that the letter came from the hospital. I also noticed that they had sent copies of it to two different places, and I thought that was strange.

I felt guilty just for having the letter in my hands, but, even so, I started to read it, as I had been ordered to do. It stated that both the mother and father of the child together had been informed that the baby had a tumour on his temple and therefore would be born physically deformed, mentally deranged, Mongoloid or all of those. I knew that such a baby's demand on the parents would be twenty-four hours a day, every minute of the day and night.

At this point, the letter fell from my hands to the floor. I was in shock! I stood there unable to move for the longest period of time. I don't know how long. Finally, I picked up the letter and put it back on the dresser, with no desire to read one more word. I had had enough. I assumed that the doctors offered them an abortion, which they had refused. Thank God!

Three days later, I felt that I was supposed to fast. I said, "Lord, how long will this fast be?"

"Twenty-one days," was the answer.

I said, "Lord, what kind of fast?"

"Same as you always do," came to me.

So, for the duration of the fast, I just drank liquids, eating no solid food. In the Word of God, it says that some come out only by prayer and fasting (see Matthew 17:21). All during my fast, the expectant parents were carrying the same heavy load in their hearts. It was painful to watch.

The day after my fast was finished, I got to their house early in the morning, as usual. I heard Kirk say, "Jalene, hurry or you'll be late for your doctor's appointment."

She answered, "I have no appointment today. Next month is my next time to see the doctor." I breathed a sigh of relief and said to myself, "Something has changed. Thank You, Lord!" From that point on to the end of the pregnancy, Jalene went to the doctor only once a month.

In the days preceding the birth, some of her relatives came to mind the children, as I had a conference to attend in Rochester, New York. Even though I went, I kept calling the house for any news. There was nothing the first day, but the next day the baby had arrived. Both the mother and the baby were fine I was told. When I think of what it could have been in this case without the prayer and fasting, all I can do is bow down at the feet of my heavenly Father and say, "Thank You!"

Today that child is doing very well. I remember a response I got from her when she was eight years old, and I was curious about her views to the future. Without a moment's pause, she said, "I will have a mansion on a hill, I will drive a Ferrari, and I will be a medical doctor."

I said, "Thank You, Lord. That's good enough for me."

～ 23 ～

A Woman Is Saved

I was walking down the street one day when a woman I knew called after me and then ran to meet me. "I want to talk to you," she explained.

"Fine," I said, "come to my shop so we can sit."

When we were comfortably seated, she began, "You have something that no one else on Queen Street has. I don't know what it is, but I wanted it. Please tell me why you are different." I told her to come to the shop at 7 o'clock that night so we could talk more freely.

She arrived at closing time, and we sat, and I told her about getting saved and assured her that the Holy Spirit could come into her life too, and what she must do.

"This is all good and fine," she said, "but I'm not ready for that." And, with that, she left.

A year later she came running into the shop one day, wanting to know when there would be a prayer meeting she could attend.

"Tonight," I said.

"Can I come?" she asked.

"Of course," I assured.

The prayer meetings were usually attended by a few people, but that night she was the only one present. She said she could only stay for a half hour, and I told her she could leave anytime she wanted.

She held my hand as I prayed, so tight I thought my fingers might break. She was crying all the time, and her nose was running, but she wouldn't let go of my hands.

She finally let go. Then she looked at her watch and said, "This time must be wrong!" I told her it was 11 P.M. "I am so sorry," she said, "I should not have done that. You are so tired." She wiped away her tears and left.

She returned to my shop for a coffee break the next afternoon and asked about the next prayer session. When she heard it was that night, she came. "I'll leave at 7:30," she said. "I won't keep you up like last night."

"Leave when you like," I said.

Again she held my hand tightly during the prayer, just as the night before, and she laughed. She was so happy that she stayed, and the hours passed. "Oh, no! I did it again," she said, upon realizing how late it was (11 P.M. AGAIN). "Please forgive me." Then she picked up her purse and walked halfway to the door. Stopping for a moment, she looked back at me and said, "Suzanne, I got what you have. I do. I really do. I got it." She was so happy and laughed in a light-hearted way. Two weeks later she moved to Vancouver.

I spoke to her several times on the telephone after that, and she said she still had the joy of the Lord and was very thankful that she had gotten saved before she left Toronto.

And I give thanks to God.

∽ 24 ∽

Dinah Is Saved from Insanity

Three of my lady friends were in my shop one morning having coffee together. One of them, Jesse, was talking about the problems her daughter, Dinah, was experiencing. She was so depressed she had even tried to commit suicide. "Since the new baby came," Jesse said, "all she does is cry. I don't understand it. Her husband is very good to her, and they have a nice house and a new car. I go and help them as much as I can."

"The baby is now three months old, but Dinah just doesn't seem to get any better." I suggested that we could all pray together for Dinah. They didn't want to say no, so they said yes, but then suddenly they all had places they needed to be, and they left.

As they were leaving, I could hear them laughing, and one commented, "Just who do you think you are?"

Silently, I said, "Lord, I am sorry. They were not laughing at me, but at You."

I later learned that Dinah had tried to commit suicide twice more and had to be hospitalized for several months. She received various kinds of treatment, but nothing seemed to work, and soon she was at home again, sitting on the sofa crying and telling herself she was "no good." So nothing had changed over the months.

One afternoon Dinah telephoned her mother and declared that she was going to kill herself, using a big knife. Her mother immediately called the son-in-law to get home, and then she called for an ambulance and the police to go to Dinah's house. So, again, Dinah ended up in hospital, tied to her bed and getting shock treatments.

About a month later, the husband was asked to meet with three specialists, who informed him that while his wife was not really physically ill, she would never be entirely cured either. They recommended that she be sent to an asylum. The husband had a difficult time with this. Dinah was just a young woman, and she was his wife and the mother of his children.

Even as the doctors talked to him, they were filling out the necessary forms to put Dinah away for the rest of her life. They then passed the forms to the husband to sign, but he refused, saying he did not have the strength to do it. He would come back later. "Take all the time you need," they said.

The husband went home and told his mother-in-law what was happening. The next day Jesse came to my shop early in the morning. She ordered a coffee but simply sat and cried. I asked her about her problem. "It's my daughter," she sobbed. "You know about her. Would you pray?" I said I would, and she left soon, without taking a single sip of her coffee.

It was two and a half years before I saw Jesse again, even though she lived within walking distance of my shop. One evening after 9 P.M. I went out walking and met her on the street. "How is Dinah?" I asked.

"Oh, didn't I tell you?" she said. "She's fine. The same week I asked you to pray, the hospital called her husband to come and get her."

Jesse said the husband had found the sudden change difficult to believe, and so he had not gone. They telephoned him again a day later, and again, he didn't go. His usual visit was on Sunday, and he went that day and saw one of the doctors in the hallway. "The doctor said his wife was fine, but he still didn't believe it," said Jesse "... that is until he went to her room and saw that she was restored as before. Needless to say, after three years of heartbreak and tears, they went home together rejoicing."

The next day Dinah phoned her boss where she used to work and asked for her job back. He said, "Come next Monday and you will have your job." Then she went and got her hair done and bought a new dress and then went home and cleaned the house from top to bottom. When her husband got home that night, the children were clean and the table was set with a hot supper she had cooked.

When I think of how close they came to such a tragic ending, all I can say is: "God never comes too late!"

~ 25 ~

Fingers Are Restored To Normal Function

I could tell something was wrong with a regular customer when he walked into my shop at 11 A.M. one day and not his usual 5 P.M. I brought him a coffee and noticed that his right hand was bandaged. "What happened?" I asked.

It was an accident at his work, he explained. He said he was using a saw and, as careful as he had been for all the years he worked there, that morning he had pushed a piece of wood into the circular saw with his hand under it as opposed to on top of it. "I lost three of my fingers," he said. "They fell to the floor, and my little finger was only holding on by a piece of skin."

He said his co-workers had picked up the fingers, packed them in ice and put them in the ambulance with him. "I went immediately into surgery, and all of my fingers have been reattached. I just came from there now."

The doctors told him he would need three more surgeries, that his middle finger would never bend again, and that it would be six months before he could return to work.

I told him to put his hand on the table so I could pray for him. He did, and I asked God to heal him.

Before he left the shop that day he said it would be two weeks before he returned to the doctor to have his hand evaluated. Some weeks later, he returned. The doctors, he explained, had changed their minds. He would no longer require more surgery, his middle finger was bending a little (although not as fully as before), and he could go back to work in six weeks. "They told me I was recovering very quickly," he said. "In fact, they called it 'a remarkable recovery.'"

And I say, with God all things are possible, if only we believe. The truth is that the compensation doctors kept repeating "remarkable recovery!" and they could not believe their eyes.

Thank You, Lord!

⌒ 26 ⌒

Kendra Is Relieved of Pain

Kendra was standing on the last step of her apartment building, right in front of the streetcar stop, as I was moving to the door to exit the streetcar. She fell and broke her foot and screamed out in pain. Three other passengers stood there with tears rolling down their faces.

Seeing what had happened, I tried to make eye contact with her. Then I said, "May I pray for you." She gave me a look that said, "Get out of my face. I have enough trouble right now without you adding to it."

A heavy wet snow was falling, and it was slippery, so I moved around to her left shoulder, so as not to trip her or touch her painful foot. Then I touched her shoulder with one finger and said one word: "Jesus!" She immediately stopped screaming and started to talk normally, and her foot was totally restored. All she had needed was one touch from the Master.

❧ 27 ❧

Alina Goes Back Home

One beautiful summer's day, a young lady walked into my shop and said to me, "I asked a man on the street where to go to get a nice cup of tea, and he told me to come here."

"I have several kinds of tea you can choose from," I replied.

She made her choice, and I got her the tea. Then she began to talk, starting with "Your place is very nice."

I thought to myself, *There is nothing nice about this place.*

"Maybe you are thinking it is peaceful," I said.

"Yes," she replied, "it's different. It's so quiet."

"It is the presence of the Holy Spirit in here," I said.

"I need to go and get my birth certificate," she told me. "Can you tell me where to go?"

"Yes. You're getting married?" I asked.

She replied with a scowl, "No, I just got out of that mess, and I'm only eighteen."

This girl was so immaculate and clean, from the top of her head to the soles of her feet. Not a single hair was out of place. Her blouse and socks and running shoes were as white as snow. I had never seen anything quite like it, certainly not on Queen Street!

Alina, as she called herself, was still drinking her tea. I said, "I feel the need to tell you a story about a sixteen-year-old girl who left home, promising never to return. She put her clothes in a pillowcase, she put the bag on her back, and then she walked to the door, saying, 'I'm sixteen now; I can do whatever I want!'

"She walked out, not even closing the door behind her or saying good-bye. Her name was Dana (not her real name).

"Dana found a place to live within walking distance of her parents' home, but from then on they never knew where she was. For the first three months that she was gone, she was drunk every single day and night. Then she lived with a married man for six months. Every Friday evening he would leave and go home to his family and come back on Sunday afternoon.

"After that she joined a gang. 'You name it, and I did it!,' she told me. 'The only thing I didn't do was kill someone.' "

Alina broke in, "Excuse me. Can I say something?"

"Of course," I answered. "You can say all you want."

"Do you see right through me?" she asked.

"No," I answered, "How do you expect me to see right through you?"

"Well, all you're saying about Dana is me!"

"Oh, I am so sorry," I said, "I'm so sorry. Please forgive me! Please!" I was in shock.

"No!" she said, "I want to hear the rest of the story."

So I continued: "The gang always had a stolen car, but they often changed vehicles. On the weekend, they did gas station and 7-11 store robberies. One man sat behind the wheel, ready to take off quickly. One man went into the station and pretended he was going there to pay at the till, while the attendant was still filling the tank. But he was there to steal from the till, and he did. In this way, they did gang robberies, and Dana said that it worked really well.

"She had several abortions. Then one day, the gang dissolved, and she found herself alone and without money. She couldn't work, for she was on drugs. At least she still had a room—for the moment.

"Unknown to Dana, she also had three Christian friends, and they were following her story, as much as they could. They knew each other from high school. They had been praying for her and they had given her name to many different Christian groups, asking them to pray for her too. So ministers and entire church groups were praying for her.

"One day three of these Christians, two men and one woman, decided to go and visit Dana. When they arrived, she curtly asked, 'What do you want?'

" 'We've come to see if you need help,' they said. 'If you say "no," we'll go home. If you say "yes," we have a plan. Please think about it for a minute. Our plan is guaranteed, and it will cost you nothing.'

"The rags the girl had on were filthy, and the place stank. She had no food and no money to buy food. The coming of this small group, therefore, was more or less like someone throwing a rope to you when you are on the lake on a cold winter day and your boat has just capsized.

"She said to them, 'Tell me what your plan is?'

" 'Our plan,' they answered, 'is that we go to a prayer meeting in a church every Thursday night. The minister prays over every one of us there, and we all pray over him and everyone that's there. You would have to do the same.'

" 'But I don't know how to pray,' she protested.

" 'We could teach you,' they assured her. 'It's very easy. We would come and get you at seven o'clock every Thursday night, and we would bring you back in our car as soon as the meeting was finished. We will do this until you find Jesus, or He finds you.'

" 'How long will that take?' she asked.

" 'We don't know,' they replied, 'but you can't stop until you find Him. You have to keep your part of the bargain if you say "yes," and we will keep our part. If you say "no," some day we will simply find you dead somewhere.'

"Fortunately she said, 'Yes,' and her Christian friends were very happy. They could not believe their ears, but they rejoiced.

"They now said, 'Would you like to go to the Dominion Store? It's not far from here. We could take you there and bring you back. You could get some groceries and maybe some clothes, and we'll pay. And you won't need to reimburse us.'

"Dana was thankful for their generosity, and she went to the store with them. (Actually, she did not have much choice.)

"Two years later she walked into my shop one day, wanting some change to do her laundry. We talked briefly. 'Have you ever seen Jesus?' she asked. 'My friends, whom I go to the prayer group with, said that if I keep searching, I'll find Him.'

" 'If you are asking me if I ever saw Jesus standing in front of me like you are now,' I answered her, 'then the answer is "no." But in my spirit I see Jesus. He speaks to me. I hear Him.'

"Then I put my hand on her shoulder and said, 'Look, Dear, when Jesus comes to you there will be no doubt in your mind that He is there, that He has come and that He will never leave you.'

"On that note, Dana ran out to go do her laundry.

"The following week she walked in, shouting, 'I found Him! I found Him!'

"Now I, too, got excited and asked, 'Where? Where? At the church?'

" 'No,' she said.

" 'At your prayer meeting on Thursday night?' I asked.

" 'No,' she answered.

" 'Where, then?' I repeated.

" 'Well,' she said, 'last week, when I was standing here at the end of your fridge, you put your hand on my shoulder. In that moment, I felt a power going into me from my shoulder all the way down to my toes. I ran out the door and knew I would never walk alone again!'

" 'I went and did my laundry. Then I ran home, and I stood by the wall where the phone was. I said, "Do I dare? No! No!" '

" 'I stayed there and debated for a while ... 'yes' ... 'no' ... 'yes' ... 'no.' Finally, I grabbed the phone and I dialed my mom's phone number, and I heard my mom's voice for the first time in several years. I said, "Mom, it's Dana! Can I come and visit you?" ' (What a shock this must have been for her mother!)

" 'Dana, dear,' she replied, 'your dad and I have stood on the porch with our arms open every night after supper, watching every girl that was coming by, hoping that it was you.'

"I said, 'Mom, I'll be there in ten minutes. I didn't take the streetcar; I ran; it was faster.' "

When I had finished telling Alina the story, the phone rang. I went behind the counter to answer the phone, but Alina followed me, crying her heart out. She was holding me tight in her arms and saying, "You will never know what you have done for me today!" Her tears were running onto my dress.

"You saved my life," she continued. "I don't need my birth certificate. I'm going back home to Mom and Dad!"

Glory be to God!

⌐ 28 ⌐

Helena, a Polish Immigrant Doctor Receives a Miracle

She was Polish and a medical doctor, but Helena was not doing very well economically in her home country. One day she said to herself, "I will go to Canada. I will open my office on a street corner in the Polish district of Toronto, and there I will do well in my practice." But it wasn't as easy as it sounded.

After she had arrived in Canada and gone to apply for a license to practice medicine, she was told she would have to write her medical exams in English. "But I don't know English well enough yet," she protested. "How long will it take me to learn?"

"At least six months," she was told.

She was infuriated by this and went to consult with a lawyer, who told her, "We cannot tell the government what to do. Besides, I know a better and faster way. In the Vienna Bakery, two doors from here, is a lady who will help you. Go and see her."

She thought to herself, *In my predicament, what could this shop owner do for me?* Nevertheless, she came to see me and sat there crying and telling me all her problems. "Now I am living on welfare," she sobbed. "I feel so degraded. My blood pressure is over 200, I have developed diabetes, and I also have other health problems. Plus, I'm crying all the time."

"Have you registered for the English course?" I asked.

"Yes," she said. "It will last six months, and every two months there will be an exam."

"Well, Helena, do your best, and God will do the rest. I will pray for you."

When she left me, she was singing, "I will do my best, and God will do the rest."

She passed her three sets of English exams, and the following month she was to have her medical exam. She thought she would be the only one there, but the large room was full of people from many nations! In her estimation, there were four hundred participants.

The exam started at twelve noon and finished at four in the afternoon. In her own words, "At twelve P.M. we started. I read the first question, and I knew the answer. I rejoiced! Some of the students rolled their paper in a ball and threw it at the teacher and then left. Others sat there and cried, while others got up and went to the washroom and vomited. We could hear them right across the hall. It was sad. I kept saying to myself, 'Suzanne is praying for me, and I will make it.'

"By three o'clock in the afternoon, I had answered all of the questions. Of course, some of my answers were wrong. Not wanting to disturb anyone, I sat there, crossed my arms, and did not move until four o'clock, when the teacher said, 'Bring your papers now, even if you only have your name on it.'

"Now we all moved into a large hallway, and some of the people were asking me, 'Why are you smiling? Why did you finish before the end of the time?'

"Because," I said, "my lady friend was praying for me. She said God would help me, and I believed her.

"Two weeks later, I got a letter that said I had passed my medical exams! I will now get my license and open my medical practice in a matter of days. When I think of how afraid I was, I am amazed that it was so easy."

I rejoice greatly and give thanks to God!

← 29 ←

Gerri Is Healed of a Brain Tumour

One evening I was at the Queensway Cathedral in Toronto. After the sermon, the pastor gave a word of knowledge. I was listening carefully, because I thought he was speaking to me. He said that someone was being healed of a brain tumour. "The tumour is pushing the eyeball out of its socket. This person is having severe headaches and often goes to a specialist," he said.

The pastor then looked around to see if anyone had responded. I got up and he called me to the front. I told him, "I believe you have described my daughter Gerri's condition."

"Is she here?" he asked.

"No, she lives in Leamington near Windsor," I told him.

"Well, she has been healed tonight," he said.

"I believe that," I assured him. "I will phone her and tell her what happened."

"Let me know," the pastor asked.

When I got home, I telephoned Gerri and told her what had taken place at my church. I added, "Next Sunday at six o'clock that same service we had will be on television. If you can be home and turn on the television, you will see and hear for yourself."

That next Monday morning I called and asked, "Well, did you watch our service on television last night?"

"Yes, Yes," she said, but did not believe it.

"Well, thank God, you are healed!" I replied.

"Yes," she answered, but I could sense that it was not wholehearted.

"You don't believe it?"

"Well, I don't see anything," she replied.

"It is not something you see," I told her. "It is something you claim." A few days later, the Lord said to her, "Call your mother and tell her you are healed."

"Yes, Yes," she responded, but she did nothing. Later in the day the Lord repeated this request. Still she did nothing about it. Then the next morning the Lord spoke to her loudly and clearly: "Telephone your mother and tell her you are healed!" This time Gerri called me and said, "The Lord told me to telephone you and tell you I am healed. So now I have done it. Bye!" And she hung up.

She still did not believe, although her headaches were gone, and when she looked in the mirror it seemed that her eyeball appeared more normal.

The following week she reported to her doctor, an eye specialist in London, a two-hour drive from her home. After an examination, he said to her, "I can't see the tumour; it's hiding somewhere. In any case, you appear all right. Make sure you come back for your next appointment."

Gerri was young in the Lord at that time, and did not have the knowledge of Him that she has now. If it was today she would simply say, "I am healed." This happened more than twenty years ago, the problem never returned, and we both praise the Lord.

⌐ 30 ⌐

Randy Is Miraculously Comforted in His Loss

In the morning news on the radio my prayer partners and I heard that Mr. Brown's home had been severely damaged by fire, and his wife and two daughters had died from smoke inhalation. The rest of the large family had gotten out safely. I sat there and prayed for the family the rest of the day.

We learned that on the evening of the fire, the oldest son, Randy, aged twenty, had a gathering with his friends in the living room after everyone else had gone to bed. The firemen said that the fire started in the sofa. The next morning the Lord gave me a vision of Randy. In the vision, he looked as though he were ninety years old. His back was hunched over, his face was all wrinkled, and every hair on his head had turned white.

I had the sense that Randy was blaming himself for the fire. He was in an agony of remorse, and my heart was aching for him. I prayed for him and for his whole family, as much as I could, day and night.

The day after the funeral the Lord gave me another vision. In this vision, the father took Randy into a large room in their house. I was wondering if the father was going to rebuke him or try to comfort him or both? They stayed in that room for hours and hours. Finally, after all that time, in my spirit I saw them coming out of the room. Randy was back to normal. There was no more white hair, no more hunched back and no more wrinkles. He had been restored to life and peace as much as was possible.

I don't know how many other intercessors the Lord had called upon to pray, not only for Randy, but for the whole family that had been so tragically tossed into this turmoil. Nevertheless, I thank God for using me in the capacity of intercessor to bring some peace to my brothers and sisters in times of sorrow and pain.

~ 31 ~

The Miracle Girl
Survives a Serious Crash

It was the first of December 1990, and I felt the Lord had just put me on a fast. I said, "Lord, how long will this fast be?"

"Seven days," was my answer.

I was thinking, *This is strange. I am fasting, but I don't know why.*

One week passed, so now I could eat. I went to the kitchen and made lunch. I put my food on the table and pulled my chair in. Then the telephone rang. It was my sister Lina.

"I would have called you before," Lina said, "but I was at the emergency for the past seven days, night and day." Guylaine, her daughter, was in a car crash at 3 A.M. one night. She missed the curb, and the car landed in the ditch. She stayed there for three hours. In Quebec, on the first of December it is very cold.

Lina said that at 6 A.M., a car passed, and the driver recognized the vehicle in the ditch, so he backed up. It was just starting to get daylight. As he got near the car and saw how badly it was damaged, he said to himself, "No one got out of there alive; that's for sure!" He got out and went down in the ditch to get a closer look.

There was a man in the front seat, and it was easy to see that he was dead. Then he spotted a girl (Guylaine) lying in the back seat, and she appeared to be very much alive. How she managed to get back there no one knew. He was shocked that anyone had escaped, but now he recognized my niece and talked to her. "Hold on!" he said. "I'll have an ambulance here for you in five minutes."

Six months prior to this accident I had spent a whole afternoon talking to Guylaine about the Lord. I told her, "If you are ever in a desperate situation of any kind, don't stand there in fear and trembling. Call on Jesus with all of your might." She had remembered those words, and each time she had seen the lights of a car passing, she would shout out as loud as she could and try to raise her arms to make a sign that could be seen through the window, but no one had seen her until daylight came. But she had also shouted out many times, "Jesus, come and help me. Jesus, come and help me."

Finally, the ambulance arrived and took her to the hospital in Drummondville. X-rays were taken, and a doctor told her, "You should be dead. I don't understand why you're still alive with the injuries you have suffered." Those injuries included a broken collar bone and pelvis and, worse, three breaks in her spine. "And yet there you are moving your legs and your arms," the doctor continued. "It's a miracle! I have never seen anything like this. The people that come here with injuries such as these are either dead or paralyzed from the neck down."

He also told her, "If you had not moved your arms and legs, trying to make signs through the window each time some car passed by, and shouted at them, I am certain you would have fainted and died."

He would, he said, do some minor repairs, but then he would have to send her on to a larger hospital in Sherbrooke.

At Sherbrooke, the doctor looked at her x-rays and he, too, was amazed by the fact that she was still alive. At first, in fact, he could not believe he was seeing the right x-rays.

"They're mine," Guylaine had to insist.

"They can't be," he said. "I'll phone the doctor in Drummondville and speak to him directly so I can get to the bottom of this."

He phoned the emergency room doctor at the Drummondville hospital, and he confirmed that these were indeed my niece's x-rays. "Do all that is in your power to save her life," he told the doctor at Sherbrooke. "This is a miracle girl!" That was saying a lot, since, in general, doctors don't like to use the word *miracle*.

It took the staff seventy-two hours of wrapping Guylaine in a hot wool blanket to stop her from shaking from the cold. For a whole week she was there one minute and fainting the next. Then came the long road to recovery. She could not walk, and her head was in a rack.

The doctor said, "When we remove this rack, if your head falls to the side, we will have to put it back in that position and leave it there for the rest of your life." Five months later, they removed the rack, and her head did not fall. Thank God! She went home and eventually had three more children.

One day Guylaine told me, "When you came to visit us and talked to me about God, I was wondering why you were saying what you said. But when I was lying in the back seat of that car, every word you said to me in the summer came back to my mind and saved my life."

Thank God!

~ 32 ~

A Baby Is Comforted

One day I was on my way back to Toronto from Montreal by train. I was on one end of the car, and mother had a crying nine-month-old baby at the other end in a stroller. She was doing everything she could to comfort the child, but all to no avail. For a while, I sat in my seat praying, but the baby kept on crying.

Finally, I said, "Lord, I will go and pay a visit to this baby. I don't seem to be accomplishing anything by sitting here and praying in my seat." So I moved toward the other end of the car.

When I got there, the baby's face was turned toward the window, but she immediately turned her head toward me, and I looked straight into her eyes. Suddenly there was not a sound coming from the child's mouth.

The mother whispered to me, "She's sick."

I kept on looking into her eyes and before long, she closed them and went off to sleep.

The mother then said to me, "You should have come and looked into her eyes sooner!"

Sometimes you need to do so very little to bless someone.

☙ 33 ☙

Sam Gets a Well-Paying Job in London

A young man named Sam walked into my shop one day and said, "I am so discouraged."

"Why?" I asked.

"Because I don't have a job, and I have no money. Now I am offered a job in London [Ontario], but I am not really qualified for it. And it doesn't pay very much. If I get there and can't do the job, then I'll have no money to come back with."

I said to him, "Go, I will pray for you, and it will be fine." And off he went.

I later learned that when Sam arrived in London his new boss introduced him to all the workers. Then he took him to his office and explained to him what he would be doing and said, "I'm sure you'll have no problems at all."

Next, he discussed his wages, which turned out to be more than Sam had expected.

"Are you able to start tomorrow morning?" the man asked.

"Yes, " Sam answered.

"Come with me, then. John will be training you. Any questions you have, ask him. He'll help you."

"Do you know your way around London," John asked him.

Sam said he did not.

Then John said, "I'll take you to a place where you can find room and board. The owners are very nice. All they ask is for you to be on time for meals and to pay when you get your cheque." Sam got a lovely large room, elegantly furnished. Six months later he came to my shop with John. I said, "You got the job in London."

He explained how well it had all worked out.

"So you came to Toronto today to do a little Christmas shopping?" I inquired.

"No," he said, "I just wanted John to meet you, because you are so different than all the other people I know. I'm so glad that I told you my problem, because I was thinking of not going to London. When you said 'go,' it made me feel better about it. Now I thank you that I have a good job."

"I thank God, and I am honored that you brought your friend to meet me," I told him.

"Now," he said, "we are getting back on the bus and going back to London."

I praise God for all His blessings.

⟿ 34 ⟾

Rika Is Healed
of a Serious Wound

It was lunchtime on a Friday at my bakery shop, and a young lady named Rika came in and ordered a coffee. She paid and took the coffee to one of my tables. Then she proceeded to take her own lunch out of her purse and eat it right there.

This was not a good precedence to set, and I felt I had to put a stop to it quickly. I started towards her, with the intention of saying something like: "This establishment is not the Salvation Army," but the Lord stopped me.

"Do you remember when you cooked potatoes for lunch and kept the peels for supper in case you had nothing else?" he asked.

"Yes, Lord, I remember," I answered.

"Do you not think that this girl could be in the same situation?"

"Okay, Lord," I answered, "I will say nothing to her."

Rika finished her lunch and left.

On the following Monday, she came back. It was then that I learned her name. This time Rika was limping.

"What happened?" I asked.

She replied, "You know last Saturday was so hot, the first hot day of spring. I ran on my bare feet in the backyard, and I stepped on a broken bottle. A piece of glass got into my foot. I was taken to the emergency department, and the doctor there sewed my foot up, and I went home. But during the night, I awoke screaming in terrible pain.

"My mom came running. She unwrapped my foot and found that it was red and very swollen, so she took me back to the emergency department."

When they got to the hospital, Rika went on to tell me, the doctor x-rayed the foot and found that there was still a piece of glass inside of it. He removed the stitches, took out the piece of glass and then sewed her foot up again, assuring her that it would be fine.

But Monday morning arrived, and Rika was not able to walk on that foot, so her mother had to call a taxi to take her to work. This taxi ride to and from work cost more than she earned, but she had no choice. Of the four people in her family, Rika was the only one with a job. The family had arrived in Canada only four months previously, and they were all depending on her to pay the rent and buy the food they needed.

At noon that day, she came to the shop again and asked for a cup of coffee. As before, she had her lunch in her purse. We talked for a while, and then I said, "Can I pray over your foot?"

She said, "Yes."

I knelt on the floor beside her, removed the rubber she had on over the bandages, put my hand under her foot and prayed. Then she went back to her work six doors up the street.

The next morning Rika came into my place on her way to work. "I came to thank you," she said. "My mom looked at my foot this morning, after she removed the bandages, and she said I was totally healed."

" 'Put your foot on the floor and see if it hurts,' she told me. "I did that, and there was no pain. So I was able to come to work on the subway. No taxi for me today. My family and I rejoice together and thank God!"

❧ 35 ❧

I Keep My Million-Dollar View

Since 1989 I've lived on the fifth floor of an apartment building, and to the southwest I have a beautiful view of Lake Ontario. In the summer, the lake is dotted with sailboats and cruisers. In the evening, when it gets dark outside, larger boats, with all of their lights, are very enjoyable to watch.

One day I was talking to a lady who lives on the sixth floor. "You must have the best view of all of these boats on the lake," I said.

"No," she said, "I only see the lake in the winter-time, when all the leaves have fallen from the trees."

I took a good look at the three trees that were in front of my window and could see that they would reach my windows in a few years and block my beautiful view of the lake. So I prayed, "Lord, please slow them down."

The following spring, I noticed that those three trees were dead. I said, "Lord, I didn't say 'kill them!'" But then the landscape men came and removed the dead trees and planted new ones in their place. But these are a different kind. They have been there now for several years, and they are growing wider, but they have stayed short. So I still have my beautiful view of all the activity on the lake, and I thank God.

My son, Jacques, calls it a million-dollar view!

⌐ 36 ⌐

Sabrina Has Her Sight Restored

One day I called my brother Camille to tell him I planned to visit with him for a few days. He and his wife live in northern Quebec. After twelve hour's ride on the bus, I arrived. And, although it was nine o'clock at night, everyone was very happy to see me.

In the morning, I was in the kitchen with Camille, and he told me that his wife Sabrina could no longer see well enough to get around or do her household chores. One of their daughters, who had never married, was living with them to care for her. Each morning, she went to her mother's room and took her to the washroom to freshen up and then to the kitchen for breakfast. After breakfast, she led her to the living room, where she spent most of her day.

The next day I was alone with Sabrina, and I said to her, "While we are alone here in the kitchen, would you like for me to pray over your eyes?"

"Yes," she said, so I prayed, and then she went to her bedroom and made her bed.

The next morning she came into the kitchen and made her own breakfast, but she never said to me, "I can see so much better now!" I don't know if she thought she had to keep it a secret for some reason. She must have at least told her daughter the same day it happened.

Several days after I got back home, I called my brother and asked him, "Has your wife told you she can see now?"

"No," he said, "she didn't, but today she dropped a little white button on the white floor, and she just bent down and picked it right up."

Every year Sabrina had an appointment with the eye specialist. On her next visit, the specialist told her, after a careful examination, that her vision had greatly improved. This was quite a turnaround. Previously the doctors had told her, "You will be blind for the rest of your life, and there's nothing more we can do. You must get used to it."

I am very thankful to God for improving her vision so much. For almost eight years after this Sabrina was able to work in her garden every summer and do her own housework. Thanks be to God!

～ 37 ～

Rambo Is Healed
of a Bleeding Wart

A six-year-old boy named Rambo had a large wart on the inside of the wrist on his left hand. It would bleed every time he hit it against something, and this would happen especially when he was playing outside with his friends. His mother had taken him to the doctor several times and tried many different remedies, but nothing seemed to work. I said to her one day when they were visiting my shop, "Would you like me to pray over his arm?"

She said, "Yes." So I prayed, and they left.

The next morning Rambo came back with his friends and said, "Miss, it's still there!"

I prayed again, and he left.

The following day he came back by himself. "Miss, it's not gone!" he said again.

"Then we'll have to pray differently," I said. "Sit here beside me, and put your arm on the table. Now, I want you to say, 'It's gone.' "

"But, Miss," he protested, "it's still there!"

"I know," I said, "but close your eyes and say, 'It's gone.' "

He did that. Then he opened his eyes and looked and said, "It's still there."

I said, "Pretend that it is gone. We are going to make believe. Now, do exactly what I say. Look at your arm and say, 'The wart is gone,' even when you see it. Never again say 'It's still there.' Do you think you will be able to do that?" He said he could.

"Very good," I said. "You can leave now. But come back tomorrow morning, and we will pray again.

"Now, what will you say when you are walking along?"

"I will say, 'It's gone,' " he said.

"Good, Rambo," I encouraged, "you may leave now. Will you be able to come tomorrow?"

"Yes," he answered and left.

Saturday morning he ran in and shouted, "Look, miss, it's gone!" And it was true. It was totally gone, and there was no trace of it ever having been there. Rambo was so happy.

I showed him the scripture in Mark 11:24 that says, *"Therefore, I say unto you what things so ever you desire when ye pray, believe that ye receive them and ye shall have them."* I thank God for his healing.

❧ 38 ❧

Ramesh Seeks the Right Wife

In 2006 I was visiting Montreal, and caught a train back home to Toronto. On the train, a gentleman from India named Ramesh came and sat with me, and we talked for a while.

I said to him, "I would like to tell you some of my stories, seeing we will be on this train for the next five hours."

He responded, "Certainly!"

When I had finished, he asked, "Would you like to hear my story?"

"I would love to," I answered. So he began:

"One day my father did not come home in the evening at the usual hour, so we thought he had met some friend and would be home later. After quite a while, when he had not arrived, my brother and I went out walking in the street, looking for him. We did not see him. He did not come home all night, and this was not like our father.

My mother thought maybe he had gotten ill, and someone had taken him to a hospital. We checked, and he was not there."

"Days turned into weeks; weeks turned into months, and our mom began to lose hope. She kept saying, 'If he were alive, he would be here.'

"One evening we were all home, the three of us, when we heard the front door open and a man came inside. He looked as though he was more than ninety years old. He had long white hair and a long white beard. He was very filthy, and his clothes were all ripped.

"My brother and I got up to tell the man that he was in the wrong house and to ask how we could help him, when suddenly he called the two of us by name."

Ramesh went on to explain that they suddenly knew this was their father. He was skin and bones, for he had been lost in the bush for the past eight months and had eaten mostly grass and the leaves of trees. Sometimes he found wild berries.

Because of the political unrest in the country at the time, they had not been able to seek help from the local police. Their father had been in politics and had been with the party kicked out when a new party took power. It was an amazing story.

We had now arrived at the train station in Toronto, and Ramesh said, "My brother and I will help you with your luggage." They walked me to the taxi stand.

"This was a most pleasant journey," he said, "You have blessed me so much. I wish I had a bouquet of roses or a box of chocolates to bless you with, but I don't." Then he pulled out his wallet and took out his only remaining bill, a twenty dollar note.

I said, "You can't give me that; it's all you have."

"It would bless me if you would take it," he insisted. "We are not short of money. My brother is here, and I will go to the bank tomorrow to get more cash."

I got into the taxi, and as he was closing the door, he said, "Please pray that I will find the right wife."

"I will," I assured him. "God bless you."

⌒ 39 ⌒

Liona's Mom Is Healed of Heart Arrhythmia

Young Liona phoned me to say that her mom was in the hospital and would have heart surgery the next day. "We can pray together right now," I said.

"No, I just came to the basement to get a jar of jam," she answered. "We're not allowed to touch the phone. I just stepped into my dad's office and used the phone here to call you. Please do pray! But I have to run now," and the line went dead.

Late in the afternoon of the next day, Liona called again. She said, "Suzanne, I told my dad I had to go to the washroom. The family has been called into my mom's room. After the surgery this morning, her heart has been racing, and they haven't been able to slow it down. They also called in the medical students to use this to teach them a lesson. They are saying she will die soon."

I told her, "Liona, we have to pray together now! Two people together in prayer is much more powerful than one." So we prayed, and she left to go back to the room.

When Liona got back to her mom's hospital room, the atmosphere had changed. She felt a peace, and her mom's heart was beating at a normal pace.

Both Liona and I are giving thanks to God!

☞ 40 ☜

John Receives a Miracle for His Heart

For many years my son John lived in northern Manitoba, 650 miles north of Winnipeg, not far from Fort Churchill, where polar bears are a way of life. One day he suffered a heart attack. A medical airplane came and took him to Winnipeg, where he underwent surgery, and three days later they sent him home.

Nine years later a doctor told John, "You need a pacemaker and another surgery before we can put in the pacemaker." John was not very thrilled about this because the equipment he used for his work would interfere with the pacemaker, so he would no longer be able to do the same work.

While all of this was happening, a word of knowledge came from Pastor Gerrie. She said, "The Lord is healing hearts now. If you have a problem with your heart, put your hand on it and claim healing." My daughter claimed a healing for her brother's heart. When she got home, she phoned me and we again claimed healing together.

Nine years later I learned that John had gone again to the hospital in Winnipeg. He had to get more tests done before any more surgeries. He was there for two days, and the needed tests were done. Then the doctor in charge told him to go home and to visit his own doctor ten days later. He would be able to pass on the results of the tests.

John was very fearful as that day approached, for these results could impact his future so greatly, and he put off going to his doctor until his wife said, "Go and get it over with." He was surprised to hear his doctor say, "Come in, John, sit down. You don't need a pacemaker or any more surgery." Several years later, he is still fine, and we thank God for it.

ᐧ 41 ᐧ

Jessica Is Healed
of Bone Cancer

In October of 2001 I went to Montreal to visit Jessica, the wife of my brother-in-law James. She was very happy to see me and proceeded to tell me that she had bone cancer. I said to her, "We can pray," but then we talked for a while. After supper, however, we did pray. She was in severe pain, and it was sad to see. A few days later, I returned home.

I telephoned Jessica, and she was pretty much the same. Then every week, for a while, when I phoned her, she reported that she was getting worse.

In November I called again, and while we were talking, the Lord impressed upon me to do an Esther fast for her. It was Monday, and I said, "Lord, I cannot start the fast before Friday night because I have to work." But my mind was made up. I was going to do it, so I did.

The following week I phoned Jessica again. This time she said that something strange had happened. "Last week, when you phoned me, while we were talking, I realized that all my pains were gone, and they have not come back since."

Still, Jessica faithfully kept all of her doctor's appointments. In April, after doing another series of tests, her doctor said to her, "The cancer is totally gone from your bones. You are no longer sick."

That day I was led to call her in the middle of the day, and I thought to myself, *Why do you phone in the afternoon when it is so much more costly?* But when she answered, she said, "You called at just the right time. I just came from the doctor, and he said that I am totally healed. Thank you very much."

Jessica is now in her nineties and is still well. Thank You, Jesus!

⌒ 42 ⌒

Prayer Blesses Bonita's Art Show

"It will be next week," Rex told me about his wife Bonita's first art showing.

"I will pray that she does well," I said.

"You never sell anything on a first showing," he replied.

"If you and I remember to pray, maybe she will," I challenged.

"I would never waste my time thinking about praying," he said. Nevertheless, on Friday, the last showing day, two of Bonita's paintings sold, and Rex and Bonita could not contain their joy. He came to the shop to tell me.

"I've come to tell you what your prayers did!" he said. "Bonita sold two of her paintings."

I think they had been down to their last dollar, and none of her paintings sold for less than a thousand dollars each. They were large paintings.

But the following week they were still at the gallery and on the next Monday an official from City Hall telephoned Bonita to say that the city wanted to purchase a series of her paintings, twenty-five in all. The best news was that the city would have a cheque ready when the paintings were picked up.

On Monday afternoon, Rex came to see me again. "I had to come tell you what your prayers have really done. We are walking on a cloud! Our feet are not touching the ground! This morning Bonita sold her series of paintings, and we now have over $30,000. From nothing at all to this! Suzanne, Bonita asked me to come and thank you," and he added, "We're now going to look for a house in the country."

I said, "Would you like me to pray?"

"Most certainly," he answered. "I am very happy for you. I thought you would be."

They found a building in the country on a large well-landscaped lot. It had been a factory, but it was in excellent condition. It had three floors and a full basement, exactly what they needed. They could live on the first floor. The second floor could be for his book business, and the third floor could be for her paintings. So, for them, it was perfect.

Their purchase offer was accepted, and they soon moved in. They could not contain their blessing and their joy. I prayed that they would always believe in prayer now.

~ 43 ~

An Electric Meter
Runs Backwards

A lady friend of mine had declared personal bankruptcy and was left with nothing and nowhere to go. I said to her, "You are welcome to come and stay with me until you find a better place."

She came, and I said to her, "Don't worry about paying every time you eat (I still had my shop at the time). When you find a job and make some money, you can give me a lump sum that you think is right, and I'll be happy with it. So then, you won't have to keep a record of what you eat every day." She was satisfied with that arrangement.

Then a whole series of things troubled me. First, I noticed that she was dressed in summer clothes and, because it was winter, she was naturally cold. I said "Put on some winter clothes."

Her answer was, "I like wearing summer dresses; they look nicer." But then she turned the thermostat up to 90° F to compensate.

She kept the light on all the time for her little dogs. "They love the light," she said. She also had electric pads she used to keep them warm. I prayed, "Oh, God, what will I do? My light bill is already as much as I can afford!"

I have two meters, one on the first floor and one on the second floor, where our living quarters are. In time, the hydro man came to read the meter, and the following week I got a bill for the first floor. "This is strange," I thought. "Before, they always sent the two bills together."

Then another man came to read the meter. I said, "They just read it last week."

"I know," he said, "but they want another reading."

A week later someone came to say that they were changing one of my meters. When I eventually got my bill for the upstairs, I found that I had been given a credit for the past two months and the next six months, and when I inquired about it, they told me that the meter had apparently gone backwards.

I say that God answered my prayers.

ᴄ 44 ᴄ

Pierre Walks Without His Crutches

My brother Pierre lived in Buffalo, New York, for more than twenty years. One day he telephoned to say he wanted to visit me, but he added, "I'm in a wheelchair. I can't walk. Will you be able to come to the bus station and get me?"

"Certainly!" I answered.

At the bus station, I found Pierre standing beside his suitcase. He had not been able to bring his wheelchair because it was too big. "I can't walk," he said. "I have to drag my feet on the floor, and I can't lift my luggage either." I told him I would get a cab and put his luggage in it and then return to help him. It took him the longest time to get across the room on his crutches.

We finally got to the door. Then there were two steps to go down, and that was a real struggle for him too. Finally, we were able to get in the taxi, and we arrived at my shop in a short time.

Once inside, we sat there like two strangers. We had not seen each other for over eleven years. We sat and talked and had a pastry and coffee.

Then Pierre asked, "Where do you sleep?"

"Upstairs," I said. "There are nineteen steps to climb."

"Oh, I won't be able to go up those stairs," he said.

"Try," I urged. "Go very slowly, and I'll walk behind you."

He made it, even though it took him half an hour. Then, once up, he said, "I won't be able to go back down."

The next morning, I was downstairs at 6:30, getting ready to open the coffee shop for business at 7 A.M. I was busy making muffins and other pastries when Pierre arrived. "I've come to wash the dishes," he announced.

"You had no problem coming downstairs?" I asked.

"No," he answered, "I even forgot my crutches and left them upstairs." The rest of the week Pierre went up and down the stairs without any problem.

That weekend two of his daughters came from Buffalo to help him get back home. They were in shock to see him walking without his crutches. They had not seen that in years. But the two of us had prayed every night together until they arrived. By then, we had experienced a snowstorm that lasted for two days, and so we now had banks of snow everywhere, some of them three feet and higher. Now, as they were getting ready to leave, Pierre carried his crutches under his left arm and his heavy suitcase in his right hand, and he actually jumped over a snow bank to get to the taxi. And I was rejoicing in the Lord!

❧ 45 ❧

I Am Healed of Phlebitis

I was walking up the stairs one day when I missed a step and struck my ankle hard against the step. My leg swelled up all the way to my hip. At first, the doctor gave me only aspirin, but when I told him, "This is not working," he did some additional tests and discovered that I had a blood clot, phlebitis and three black spots on my ankle. It was so painful that I could not even endure having a sheet on my leg.

The doctor decided that he needed to operate. "Think about it," he said, "and when you are ready, give me a call. But don't waste time. You have gangrene. This is very serious."

I went home and prayed for three days. On the third day, I was kneeling down in my room praying, and 'Vitamin E' kept coming to my mind. Then I heard, "You have a book about the benefits of taking Vitamin E."

I got up and found the book, and I started to take Vitamin E, as it recommended. Still, nothing was happening.

I read some more of the book and found that it said, "If you don't take enough Vitamin E, nothing will happen." So, I began taking four capsules a day instead of the two I was already taking. Two days later, when I woke up in the morning, the swelling was gone totally out of my leg, the black spots were gone, and there was no more pain in my leg. The Vitamin E was coming out of my body through my navel, and it stank like rotten meat, but I knew that my life was no longer in danger.

I had made an appointment to see a specialist (there was a doctors' strike at the time, and I had never heard of that before). When I finally got to the specialist, who was in a different city, he said, "Tell me all of what took place." So I did.

When I had finished, he said, "If you had not taken the Vitamin E when you did, you would be in hospital now and in big trouble."

I thank God that He impressed upon me to take the Vitamin E, which saved my leg and possibly my life. And I thank God for taking care of me, even more than I realized.

This happened many years ago, and I never had problems with my legs again. Of course, that doctor told me to take Vitamin E every day for the rest of my life. Thank You, Lord!

ॐ 46 ॐ

Mary Anne Receives God's Help with a Difficult Court Case

A few years ago, I was invited to the home of Pierre and Mary Anne, my younger son and his wife, one evening for supper. It was a Sunday, and when I arrived Pierre was in the kitchen preparing the food.

"Where's Mary Anne?" I asked.

"At work," he said, "She'll be here soon."

"What do you mean, at work? Today is Sunday."

"I know. But she's preparing her court case."

Mary Anne is a lawyer, working for a large electrical utility. During a two-month period she had often gone to work at 6 in the morning and not returned until 7 that evening. She was supposed to have another lawyer working with her, but she was told there was simply no one available, so she was on her own. Considering that the other side in this particular case had three lawyers, "One could get a little nervous," she told me later when she eventually appeared.

When I was getting ready to go home that evening, she said to me, "You can try your prayers on my court case, if you like." I was a little surprised, not knowing for sure how much Mary Anne believed in my prayers. Nevertheless, I told her I would pray.

She said, "The lawyers on the opposite side are as smart as I am, or better. That's the reason they're there. And if you lose too many cases, you could find yourself walking the streets, looking for a job." I could feel her concern.

Later, at home I prayed, "Lord, I know very little about this case, so it makes it difficult to know exactly how to pray."

I did know that there was a large building, valued in the millions of dollars, that had been empty for several years. The owner had long been trying to sell it, but hadn't been able to. Then one day the building was levelled in a fire. The owner subsequently claimed the insurance money, and the insurance company was unable to prove in court their suspicions, that the fire had been set on purpose by the owner to collect the insurance money. Many rumors were going around that it was arson, but the insurance company had to pay up.

Then, after several years had passed, the insurance company, wanting to retrieve the money they had been forced to pay out, decided to take the electric company to court, claiming that the fire had been caused by faulty wiring. According to them, the electrical inspector had been negligent at the time of the wiring of the building, and so the building had burned on its own. They seemed to ignore the fact that the building had stood firm for several decades without a problem.

Anyway, I started to pray, "Lord, I don't know who is right in this case, but I ask You, if the insurance company is wrong in putting in this claim, that You would confuse their lawyers so much they will not know their heads from their feet." That's all I knew to pray.

The court date finally arrived. Three male lawyers represented the plaintiff, so they started expounding their case. However, they suddenly seemed to be missing an important paper. Then they were getting hot; their faces were red. They took off their coats; their shirts were wet with perspiration. Still, they were unable to locate the missing paper. They approached the bench and asked the judge for a ten-minute recess. Surprisingly, he said, "No," and then he took the gavel, hit the desktop, and pronounced, "Case dismissed!" And that was it.

Mary Anne stood up, put her papers in her briefcase, and returned to her office. She met her boss in the hallway as she was going in. "What are you doing here, Mary Anne?" he asked. "Were you not supposed to be in court this morning?"

"I was," she told him. "We won!"

"It's only five after eleven," he responded. "I was under the impression this court case would last a week!"

"It was supposed to," she answered. "The case was dismissed."

I was sure that God had done a miracle in answer to my prayer. Praise God!

～ 47 ～

A Crying Newborn Is Comforted

In 2003 I was invited by the End-Time Hand-maidens to attend their conference in Regina, Saskatchewan. I got on the plane and went. Five days later, the conference was over, and I called a cab and went to the airport for my flight home.

After the plane got into the air, a little baby started to cry and would not stop, no matter what the parents did. I sat there and prayed, but nothing changed. I decided to go see what could be done.

The father had the baby in his arms, and it looked like it was no more than a week old. I said, "Perhaps the pressure in the cabin, as we went up, caused pain in his ears."

The baby was still crying, so I asked if I could take him in my arms. The mother shouted to the father, "What did she say?"

"She asked if she could take the baby in her arms," he said.

"I guess so," she answered.

As soon as the baby was in my arms, he fell asleep. The four other little brothers and sisters shouted, "Mom, the baby stopped crying!"

Thanks be to God.

❧ 48 ❧

Freddi Is Healed of Torn Ligaments

It was the 14th of September 2010, and I was just beginning a train trip to Chatham from Toronto. I got to the train station but then got on the wrong elevator. Then I got to a track that had no train on it. A VIA rail employee rescued me and took me to my train.

"There are no more seats here by the window," I was told, "but if you want to go to the very end of the car, you may find one." I did, and there was a family sitting with four seats, two each facing one another.

One lady was already there, so I sat with her. Fifteen minutes later, the train stopped in Oakville, and a man and his wife got on. They had to walk from one end of the car to the other, and she was having a hard time walking on her crutches with the train already moving. We later learned that she had ripped

all of the ligaments in her foot, and it was very painful, so bad that the doctor had to put a cast on it.

As they arrived at the end of the car, her husband
said, "At least, dear, we did find a seat."

I said, "And you have the best seat in the car!"

Freddi was her name, and she was a little dis-
turbed at my statement. She raised her voice a bit
and said, "Why is this seat that I have the best seat
in the car?"

"It's because you have hurt your foot," I said,
"and now, the best thing for you to do is to put your
foot up on the seat here beside me. Then I will put my
hands on your foot and pray." (She had already had
her foot propped up on a chair for ten days at home!)

Her husband said, "Yeah, this is what my mom
would say."

"I do this all the time," I said, "and if you don't
believe me, I can give you a story to read. I have
some right here in my briefcase which I am taking to
my favourite son-in-law for editing."

Freddi said, "You have a favourite son-in-law,"
and her tone of voice was sort of like a question.
After a few moments, her husband said, "Calm
down, dear, she has only one son-in-law." We all
had a good laugh.

I gave them each a story to read. When they were
finished, the husband looked at me and said, "Did
you know that this is a miracle?"

I said, "All of my stories are miracles or else they would not be in my book."

"Do you have more stories? Can we get another one to read now?"

After they finished reading the second story, they said, "Would you write our address and phone number down and call us when the book is ready? We want a copy of that book."

Then I had reached my destination, so I got off the train. Freddi and her husband were going on to the United States. Three weeks later I telephoned their house, and they were back.

"Suzanne, I am so happy you called," said Freddi. "I have something to tell you. When we left you, we crossed the border and went to our hotel. In the morning, when I woke up, I said to my husband, 'My foot is not hurting. I think I will put my foot on the floor.' He warned me not to, and reiterated what the doctor had cautioned, but I said I would be careful.

"I did it, and I didn't feel any pain. Then I said, 'I will put a bit of pressure on it and see how that feels.' When that didn't hurt, I said, "I'll try to stand up on my feet.' "

" 'Oh, no, dear! Don't do that. It's too dangerous,' my husband said. Nevertheless, I stood up and took a step. And I have been walking ever since!

"After all that, I went to the doctor, and he was

very surprised to see me walking. He took the cast off. When he examined the foot, it was no longer swollen, not even red. In fact it was totally restored, and he didn't expect that.

"The doctor then said, 'It should have taken at least three more weeks. I don't understand!' "

But God understood.

∾ 49 ∾

Murillo Has a Prosperous Year in University

"But, Murillo, why are you planning to go so far to attend university?" I asked. "We have an excellent university right here in Toronto, and great libraries as well. It would cost you much less to stay here at your parents' house."

"I'm not going there to come back home with an 'A' on my report card, like a good little boy," he said. "I'm going there to have fun, and fun I will have! I assure you that I will fail my year at the university, but my father will not be behind me every time my hand touches the door handle to ask, 'Murillo, where are you going?' "

As I stood there listening to this young man, I was shocked. I knew his parents, and they were working very hard to raise their family successfully. Murillo was now giving me the impression that he was planning to get at least three girls pregnant, smash no fewer than two cars, and get drunk every weekend.

After a while he had left my shop, and no sooner had the door closed behind him than I said, "Lord, stop him dead in his tracks. Put a true born-again Christian on his trail, and don't let him escape" (see John 3:3).

In time, Murillo arrived at the university in Thunder Bay. At the office, he had a big debate with the clerk, Lina. He said, "I want room number 7."

She replied, "I already gave out that room before you got here. There are two tenants in it, a boy and a girl." Instead, she offered him room number 10. He went to room number 10, but he was still lamenting and complaining. The next day he had a note in his mailbox that said, "Murillo, come to the office."

He arrived at the office, and Lina said to him, "I was finally able to remove the girl from room 7. Here's the key. You can move in there now."

Murillo was excited. He said, "I will wash your car. I will go do your grocery shopping. I will kiss your feet. I will not ask you for anything for the rest of the year." In this way, Murillo moved in with a boy named Tim.

It was Tim's second year to be in this room, and after introduction, he said, "Anything you want to know, just ask me. I'll help you any way I can. We'll be going for supper in a few minutes. So come with me, and I'll show you where the dining room is. Then, after supper, we'll go to the prayer room to pray for fifteen minutes. We have been granted a free room for the whole year, and it is most excellent! Every night we go there to pray, and in the morning we pray too, but only for ten minutes."

Murillo was stunned and said, "I don't pray."

Tim said, "Man, if you live in my room, you *will* pray!"

"I don't know how to pray," Murillo protested, "and I don't pray out loud."

"We will teach you how to pray (there will be ten of us altogether), and anybody can pray out loud," he was told.

About then, Murillo was not a happy camper. Surely this had not been in his plan. Nevertheless his presence was required, and when it came his turn to pray, Tim elbowed him in the side and said, "Your turn."

Murillo answered, "I don't know what to say."

"Surely you can say, 'Praise the Lord,' Tim encouraged. So that's what Murillo did.

Tim prayed next, and the prayer went on around the circle until everyone had prayed several times in the fifteen minutes allotted. About then Murillo posed a question to himself: "How on earth did I get into this mess?" It was as though he had set his own ambush, and now he was trapped in it. He surely could not go back to the office and say, "I want to move out of that room." Certainly not, after the promise he had made to Lina. I'm also sure that Tim had requested from the other eight students that they pray fervently every day for Murillo's successful year. From my shop in Toronto, I was also praying for him, that God would give him great diligence.

Finally, school was over for the year, and Murillo came home. His mother asked for his report card. "The school will mail it," he replied. A month later his report arrived in the mail, and his mother read it carefully. She said to the father, "This is *not* Murillo's report. They've made a mistake. They will surely realize the mistake, and they'll correct it and send us another report."

When nothing else came, they finally called the university and complained, and someone in the office there said they would get back to them within two days. When the call came, the university representative said, "We have checked carefully, and the report we sent is indeed your son's report."

The parents still couldn't believe their ears. They could not understand. Not only had Murillo passed his courses; he had an excellent report!

Thank God, prayers never fail.

～ 50 ～

My Four Prayer Requests Are Answered in One Day

In the summer of 2004 I was preparing to go to a retreat in Orleans, Ontario, near Ottawa, and I prayed, "Lord, I'm asking You for four things, which I need today. First, I want someone to sit beside me on the train who would like to hear about You, and that he (or she) would listen to what I have to say. Two, I ask You, Lord, to give me a ride from the train station to the retreat at the convent. Three, I also want to see my friend Kathleen. And, four, I need a ride to the restaurant because the day we arrive no food will be prepared for us."

I was in my seat on the train, and along came a Moslem man. When he got near my seat, it was as if someone had given him a push, for he literally fell into the seat beside me. I was thinking an angel had pushed him. He said, "I guess this is where I sit?"

I said, "That is fine with me."

He proceeded to open his briefcase and start working. With his left hand he was propping one eye open, and with the other hand he was writing on some papers.

I was reflecting to myself, "Lord, how do I get his attention?"

As he was flipping the page, I said, "Sir, you are very tired I see?" He immediately put his pen back in his shirt pocket, his papers back into his briefcase and proceeded to tell me about his work. He was a professor at the University of Ottawa, where he taught the teaching staff about financial investment. He was flying out of Ottawa that night for India.

"Where are *you* going?" he then asked.

"I'm on my way to Orleans," I answered.

"Oh, no, you are kidding?" he responded.

"No," I said, "that is where I am going."

"You are visiting your family there?" he asked.

"No," I told him, "I am attending a retreat sponsored by the Evangelical Sisterhood of Mary from Darmstadt, Germany."

"Orleans is where I live," he said. "How do you get from the train station to Orleans?"

"By buses," I answered.

"Well, that takes you a long time to get there," he said.

"Yes," I responded, "because the buses stop often, and also because I have to change buses twice."

"If you would like," he said, "I could give you a ride to Orleans from the train station. My car is parked there."

I asked him if he had family in Ottawa, and he said, "Yes, my daughter is a student at the university where I work, and my son is at the high school where my wife teaches."

He asked me, "Have you gone to this place before by car from the train station?"

I said I had.

"Then you will probably remember some part of the way," he said.

Since he had told me he was leaving for India that very night, I said, "Yes, that is possible. But sir, I don't want to waste your time, seeing you are getting on the plane to India at 7 o'clock tonight."

I was surprised by his answer: "If I miss my plane tonight, there will be another one tomorrow." And he took me right to the door of the Retreat House.

We had been together on the train for almost five hours from Toronto to Ottawa, and I had shared with him some of my stories of answered prayer. He said to me, "Your stories are very powerful! I have never heard anything like this before."

"It is the power of God," I said.

"I believe you," he answered, "and it is not a co-incidence that I sat with you, for I would like to ask you to pray for one of my friends."

"Fine," I said. "I will." And he told me this story.

"Twenty years ago my friend C.P. and I were invited to a wedding. The celebration was in the evening. I said to C.P., 'I will pick you up with my little truck.' We did not have phones like we do now. When the wedding day arrived, I got in my pickup and went to C.P.'s house, only to learn that he had bought a motorcycle and wanted to try it out. I said, 'Fine! I'll see you at the wedding.' And I left.

"All that evening I kept looking for C.P., but he didn't arrive. The next day I was told that he had suffered an accident. His motorcycle had hit a hydro pole, the pole and the wire broke, and he was in the hospital.

"As a result of the accident, one of C.P.'s arms was severely burnt to a crisp from the shoulder to the tip of the fingers, and he has never been able to use it since that time. Would you pray for him? And then would you give me your phone number so I can let you know if there is any change?" I never again heard from this man, and I am still praying for C.P.

But the Lord had granted my four requests. First, the professor had sat beside me and listened to what I had to say about the Lord, and he agreed. Second, I had asked the Lord for a ride from the train station to the retreat at the convent and He granted me that. Third, when I arrived at the retreat house, I met Kathleen in the hallway and was pleased to see that she had come.

My last request was a ride to the restaurant. I was in my room, and I decided to go for a walk in the hallway. The convent was huge, and as I was walking along, a door opened in front of me, and out walked my friend Bernice. She said, "Suzanne, we are going to the restaurant. Would you like to come with us?"

I said, "That is an answer to my prayers! Thank You, Lord, for granting my four requests today."

～ 51 ～

Kari Is Saved in Time

Kari, a fifteen-year-old, had been admitted to the Toronto Western Hospital with a severe case of leukemia, but his parents lived three hours away. They came every weekend to see him, and his born-again sister, Dee, also came with them and prayed for him. I knew all of this because I saw his nurse, Doris, at church sometimes. She was also born again, and we prayed together at the church.

One day Doris said to me, "Suzanne, we'll have to pray harder or pray more, because he's losing ground. His vision is going, and every day he has more hearing difficulty. I have never met his parents, but I can feel their pain. Kari will be just sixteen years old a few days from now."

Because I know that two persons praying together is more powerful than one praying alone, on

Wednesday evening I phoned my young teenage friend Gail. "Gail," I said, "what are you doing?"

"Nothing," she answered. "I'll be over in less than five minutes."

She came in very excited and asked, "Who are we praying for today?"

"We are praying for Kari," I told her, and we sat down and began to pray.

After a little while, Gail shouted, "Suzanne, I heard some words!"

"What did those words say?" I asked.

She replied, "I heard, 'Let Kari receive the Lord.' "

I shouted, "Praise the Lord! He has gotten saved!"

Gail told me, "It's the first time in my life that I've heard words like this!"

"Well, it will not be the last," I told her. "You will hear them again. The Lord will speak to you from time to time in this way."

That same evening at the hospital, Kari asked a nurse to call his girlfriend Lola from the floor above to come down. The nurse said, "She's working." (Lola, the same age as Kari, was in training to become a nurse).

"Yes, I know," he said, "but I only want to see her for five minutes."

Seeing that he was dying, the nurse agreed to call Lola, and she came.

Standing in the doorway to his room, Lola said, "Kari, I'm here. What did you want?"

"Don't just stand there," he said. "I can't see you from where you are. Come here and sit on the bed beside me." So Lola sat down beside him on the bed.

Kari proceeded to hug and kiss her and he laughed and laughed and then hugged and kissed her some more. This went on for some five minutes.

Then she asked, "Kari, what did you call me for? What do you want?"

"That's all I wanted," he said. "You can leave now if you wish."

After praying with Gail, I phoned Doris at her home. She was sleeping already. I left a message with the other girls there that Kari had gotten saved on Wednesday early in the evening.

The next morning Doris went to the phone to see if there were any messages for her from the hospital. Thursday was her day off, but sometimes the hospital needed her and would call and change her day off to another day or change her work hours as needed. There was no message from the hospital, but she did get my message.

She was so excited that immediately she put on her uniform and her work shoes and ran to the hospital, not even waiting for the streetcar. She did not even wash her face or brush her teeth; there was no time for that.

When she arrived in the hallway where Kari's room was, she felt the power of God. She bounced into his room to find that the joy of the Lord was upon him. His face as radiant as sunshine. He was still laughing and rejoicing in the Lord. The staff members who did not know the Lord were saying that he had lost his mind. "How sad!" "It was bound to happen!" "He has gone insane."

Those who knew the Lord said, "Praise God, he's gotten saved!"

On Friday his parents came. They were also sure that he had lost his mind, but his sister Dee knew the truth, that he had received the Lord. On Saturday, at six o'clock in the afternoon, Kari passed away, to be in the presence of the Lord.

Thank You, Jesus!

🢒 52 🢐

An Accountant Sees God's Hand at Work

I was taking the train home from Ottawa when a young man came and sat beside me. As usual, I wanted to talk to him about God and his salvation, since, to me, there is nothing more important in the world. But try as I may, nothing was happening. He just kept on reading his book, which was about two inches thick.

I was getting a little vexed because I was unable to put in a word, and finally I said to myself, "I will win this battle one way or another," and I started to pray. Within a few minutes, the young man put down his book and began to talk to me.

He said he had gone to Ottawa to visit his mom and dad, and now was heading home to Toronto, where he worked as an accountant. "My employer gave me this book to read," he said, "and said I should finish reading it by Monday morning."

He explained that when the train arrived at Union Station it would be midnight. Then he would have to take the subway to the end of the line, then a bus to the end of its route and then walk a mile more to get home. "I have two more hours of reading to finish the book," he said. "Tonight I will have very little time to sleep, if any." And, with that, he picked up the book and began reading again.

Soon we arrived at Union Station. "I don't believe it," he said, getting to his feet. "I knew it was an impossible task. I just don't get it."

I stood up and said to him, "Prayers always work."

"Hmmm," was his only response.

He asked if someone was coming to get me.

"No," I replied, and when he asked where I lived I told him in the west end.

"Get home safely," he said, and then hugged me and said good-night.

"It was very nice meeting you," I said, "and I am happy you finished reading your book."

"Yep," he said, "I got through it all. Not sure how, but it's done, and now I can get to bed when I get home."

He left, and I then thanked God for answering another prayer.

☞ 53 ☜

God's Presence Is Felt in the Vienna Bakery

Late one afternoon a gentleman came into the shop. He was dressed in a suit, white shirt and necktie, suggesting that he was not from Queen Street. He sat down and ordered a coffee, and then, after finishing the coffee, he got up and left.

He then drove to his home, far in the north of Toronto, and when he had gotten into the house, he asked his wife, "Have you ever been in the Vienna Bakery on Queen Street?"

"No," she answered.

"Well, I want you to go there tomorrow," he said.

"Why?" she asked. "It's so far. What would I go there for?"

"Well, ... ," he ventured, "buy a cake for Sunday. And then I want you to tell me what is in that place."

"Well, if you were there, you should know," she said.

"That's the problem," he reported. "I can't figure it out. I have never been in a place like that in all my life."

So the woman came in the next day and said to me, "My husband was here last night, and he wants to know what's in your place?"

I said, "What do you think?"

"I feel that it's the Holy Spirit," she answered. "The presence of the Lord is certainly here."

I said to her, "Last year a woman came in for coffee, and she was here only a short time. After she got home, she phoned me and said, 'Suzanne, I saw the Lord in your shop today. Do you believe me?' I said, 'I certainly do.' "

It was wintertime, and there was snow and ice on the roads and sidewalks, and it was cold outside. Nevertheless, the lady had come, and she was very happy that she now had the answer to the mystery her husband had posed.

From time to time, customers asked me similar questions: "Why is it so peaceful in your place?"

There was only one answer. It was *the peace of God, which surpasses all understanding*" (Philippians 4:7, NKJV).

And I gave praise to God, pleased to know that some people noticed the difference!

∽ 54 ∽

Anna Is Delivered from Alcoholism

Every year I go to visit my two sisters in Drummondville, Quebec. They don't come to me, because they are not bilingual and believe it would be impossible for them to make their way in the English world of Toronto. They are several years younger than I and live together in the countryside.

One day I was talking to one of them, Lina, about the Lord. She owns the house they live in. I was trying to convince Lina that she would have more peace and more joy if she surrendered to God. I explained to her about the manna we read about in the Bible and shared with her this testimony.

Two pastors, a couple, had come to our church. After having stood at the altar worshiping, he sat down, and suddenly his hand was full of manna. It was, in appearance, much like a cracker, smaller than a quarter of an inch in size. He served it to the thirty-five of us present in communion, and so each of us tasted it, and still there was much left over. He gave some to our pastors and asked if anyone else wanted some. I said, "I do," so he gave me some on a tissue.

I put it in a little jar at home and carried it with me everywhere I went, giving some to everyone I ministered to. For instance, I gave some to one of my nieces, Anna. Anna was an alcoholic and had been for several years, and she was drunk at the time I ministered to her. I questioned myself, "Why am I doing this?" but I hoped against all hope that she would be saved. I knew that she was living a miserable life.

I said to Anna, "If you would invite Jesus into your heart, He would help you." To my amazed surprise, she did! I wanted to shout and scream, "Alleluia!" but seeing her intoxicated condition, I restrained myself, not knowing what, if anything, would happen next. I was holding my breath and saying, "Lord, you have to do it!" and "Don't let her escape!"

Anna went back to the swimming pool outside with her bottle of beer. Her common-law husband, Ron, came in to get a cold beer from the fridge, and I said to him, "Someday the Lord will deliver you from that."

He looked at me and said, "Why not now?"

"If you are ready," I told him, "I can pray with you right now."

He sat by the table, and I sat on the other side. "You will have to let go of the bottle," I said, "because I am going to hold your hands." I took them both and held on tightly as I prayed, and he repeated the prayer after me. Then he started to cry out loud and said, "Where is the washroom?"

"On your left down the hall," I said.

He was crying in the washroom for the next half hour. Then he went back to the swimming pool. Not long after that, he and Anna left.

When he got home, he said to his Uncle Joe, "I want you to meet my Aunt Suzanne from Toronto. I'll take you there tomorrow."

The next day, after lunch, Ron and Anna arrived, with three of Ron's sons, her four children, Uncle Joe and (of course) their bottles of beer.

No one introduced me to Uncle Joe. After a while, he and Ron's three boys came into the house, while the rest stayed out by the pool. I was planning to sit in the big chair in the living room, to talk to the boys, but the uncle got to the chair before me. He sat down and pulled his hat over his eyes, as though he was planning to sleep. He looked old and tired.

I said to the boys, "Let's go down to the basement. I would like to talk to you about Jesus." Their ages were eight, ten and twelve. We sat down and the uncle came down behind us. I didn't know why he was following us, not knowing that Ron had talked to him about me. He went and got a chair and sat beside me.

I led the boys to the Lord, one at a time. They were very attentive, and it was amazing to see how they clung to every word I said.

When I had finished, the uncle started to cry and said, "I have been living in this Canada for eighty-two years, and how is it that not one person has ever come to me and talked the way you talked to these boys?"

I said, "Would you also like to give your heart to the Lord?"

"Yes, I would," he affirmed. He did, with tears rolling down his face. I was so thankful to God! I couldn't contain my joy.

Two days later, one of my sister Lina's step-sons, Don, came with his wife Olive. They were to have supper with us. While Lina was preparing the food, I was talking to the couple about God and about the manna. The son responded, just as his father had, "There is no God and no manna, and I don't want to waste my time talking about things that don't exist."

My little jar of manna was there on the table with just a few crumbs left in it. I asked his wife, Olive, if she would like to taste it. She said "Yes."

I gave her some. There was just a little crumb in the spoon left over. I poured it into the spoon and offered it to him. Surprisingly, he took it.

I closed the jar tightly, left it on the table and watched it. A few minutes later, Don said, "The jar was empty, so why are there four little crackers in it now?" We were all surprised, but it was true. There was more manna in the jar!

Don and Olive were more in shock than surprise. The rest of the evening Don kept shaking his head and never said another word. He had no answer for this phenomenon. But I rejoice in the Lord for it!

My vacation came to an end, and I returned home to Toronto on the train. A week later, I phoned my niece, Anna. She answered the phone in a normal voice, which I was happy to hear. A month later, I phoned her again. She said, "Am I ever happy to hear your voice! No one calls me except my mom." I realized she was no longer drinking. This year, on my annual trip, I went to visit her at her house. Anna is no longer an alcoholic. The quality of her life has improved greatly. And I give thanks to God!

Her four children are all so thankful that their mother is sober 24 hours a day.

Lord, thank You!

⚬ 55 ⚬

Gene Is Healed from a Botched Surgery)

One day a lady friend of mine phoned me from the law firm where she worked. She said, "Suzanne, I am going to ask you for a favour. You know that everything that is said between the lawyer and his client is secret."

I said, "Yes."

She replied, "I will have to say a few words, just enough for you to understand what to pray about. This young man got married, and he and his wife were preparing to have a family. They already had a long list of boys' names and girls' names. One night, Gene woke up with severe pain in his back. They went to the emergency room. Several hours later, he was diagnosed with kidney stones and was told he needed surgery. He had the surgery, and he started to recover.

"But he still did not feel good. He was thinking, 'This whole thing was a mess, like a botched job.' He couldn't understand it.

"He went to the family doctor, and the doctor confirmed his fears. He said, 'This was not a surgery; it was an atrocity. You will never be able to father a child.'

"Gene and his wife were in each other's arms, crying in desperation. Then Gene took off in a rage. He went to the lawyer's office and laid a heavy charge on the doctor who had performed the operation on him.

"So, Suzanne, could you please pray for him?" my friend asked. And I did, hoping as I prayed.

A month later, I went to a conference in Toronto. Two evangelists came from the States for three days. On the last day, one of them said, "I have a vision from the Lord for a young man here. You went and had a surgery for a kidney stone."

I thought to myself, "The man he is talking about is a Moslem; he is not in this meeting. He would not attend this type of meeting." I know that this message was for me to pray and to claim healing for this man. The evangelist was seeing (in the Spirit) the actual surgery taking place in the operating room. He said, trembling, "I have never seen anything so brutal. It is a horror scene. It is not the knife of a surgeon but that of a butcher. But the Lord is saying to you, Young man, 'Trust in the Lord. He will see you through.' "

I wanted to scream at the top of my lungs, "Thank You, Jesus!" I was so happy that he spoke those words! It felt like it was a setup from God.

Six weeks later the lady from the lawyer's office phoned me again. She said, "Suzanne, the young man came back to lower the fine he put on the doctor. He says his health is being restored."

Glory to God!

Your Opportunity

Now that I have come to the end of my book, I do not want to leave you without giving you an opportunity to surrender your life to God, which is the most important thing you can do in this world. Sincerely repent and ask Jesus to forgive you of your sins. Such repentance is a habit to be developed in us daily so that our prayers are answered, so that we are clean vessels. Thank God for shedding His blood on the cross for you and now taking up residence in your life.

If you have prayed this prayer, welcome to a lifetime of adventure.